2.97

HOW TO SUCCEED AS AN ARTIST IN YOUR HOME TOWN

STEWART BIEHL

NORTH LIGHT BOOKS

Cincinnati, Ohio

How to Succeed as an Artist in Your Hometown. Copyright © 1990 by Stewart Biehl. Printed and bound in Hong Kong. All rights reserved. No part of this book may be reproduced in any form or by any electronic or mechanical means including information storage and retrieval systems without permission in writing from the publisher, except by a reviewer, who may quote brief passages in a review. Published by North Light Books, an imprint of F&W Publications, Inc., 1507 Dana Avenue, Cincinnati, Ohio 45207. First edition.

94 93 92 91 90   5 4 3 2 1

Library of Congress Cataloging in Publication Data

Biehl, Stewart
      How to succeed as an artist in your hometown / Stewart Biehl.
            p.   cm.
      Includes bibliographical references and index.
      ISBN 0-89134-357-1
      1. Water-color painting—Vocational guidance.   I. Title.
ND2130.B53   1990
751.42'2'068—dc20   90-7636
                                                     CIP

Edited by Linda Sanders
Designed by Cathleen Norz

Cover photograph by Ron Forth

Dedication

To Grace, my patient and understanding wife and partner of fifty years, who does so much more than just being there. Her love, confidence, and encouragement made this book possible. A special thank you is also due to the other two women in my life, daughters Patricia and Pamela, for their interest and support.

Acknowledgments

With gratitude…

To David Lewis, editorial director at North Light Books, for his faith in this project and his ongoing encouragement…he believed I could do it.

To Linda Sanders, my editor, who also said, "Yes you can" and then patiently guided this project to its conclusion… she brought it all together.

To the staff at North Light, truly a great team of professionals… always ready to help.

To the fellow artists who graciously permitted me to show their work and tell their stories.

A special debt of gratitude is owed to the owners of my paintings reproduced in this book, and a special thank you is extended to all patrons who have purchased my paintings these many years. Their encouragement and support is most gratifying.

CONTENTS

CHAPTER 1

What You Need to Paint

CHAPTER 2

In the Studio

CHAPTER 3

Growing as an Artist

CHAPTER 4

Deciding What to Paint

CHAPTER 5

How to Please the Small Town Buyer

Dusk Settles on St. John's,
14¼ x 21¼ inches,
watercolor.
Collection of the artist.

*One of the best reasons to paint is
the personal satisfaction it brings.
This painting was the final
acceptance I needed to be elected a
signatory member of the Pennsylvania Watercolor Society; it will
remain in my personal collection.*

INTRODUCTION

Some time ago the publishers of North Light Books suggested that I consider doing a book on watercolor painting by Joe Average. First I laughed out loud and second I responded, "No way!" I'm still deeply involved in the learning process. I looked at the books on watercolor in my library by Tony Couch, Zoltan Szabo, Everett Draper, Phil Austin, and so many more, and I cringed. What in the world could I say or offer that has not been presented before? These artists are all members of the American Watercolor Society and more! I'm just Joe Average.

"That's just the point we want to make," I was told. "We'd like to present the thoughts and work of Joe and JoAnn Average. We'd like to let the J. Averages in the world know that they can survive and grow." Of course no one is truly average because each person has something special to offer, but this book would be written for the ordinary hard-working artists out there who are serious, but are working outside the limelight of big cities or famous galleries.

So I started to do some thinking. There are thousands of watercolorists out there and every one dreams of becoming a signatory member of AWS (the ultimate recognition), but how many make it? Possibly five hundred to six hundred. The chances of reaching that elitist plateau are very slim. But even if we never reach that level, we part-time painters still fantasize about making a living from our art and we are hungry for information that will help us to do so. We dream—perhaps we'll never make a full living from our art—but we dream.

Dreams alone won't do it. As part-time painters, we face difficult issues. Not everyone wants to give up that paying job, with its often most attractive (and growing) benefits. Can't you continue your present vocation—maybe it's even art related—and still enjoy a serious pursuit of art? Of course you can.

Is there a certain plateau you must reach before you can sell your work? Must you live in a metropolitan area with art schools and art centers and galleries and sophisticated clientele in order to sell your work? Can't you live in your small town or rural area and paint and sell your work as you grow? Sure you can!

So I decided to write this book to help painters like me deal with the special problems and challenges we face. One person's success stories can be very helpful to others who are in similar circumstances. So why not share them?

The thrust of this book is to help Joe and JoAnn Average produce paintings that will attract customers from "Main Street America"—customers not art trained, but who do appreciate an image that is familiar or pleasing to them.

Eric Sloane said it all: "The powers that be today—those galleries that are more apt to sell prestige than art, and the critics whose abstract rhetoric conjures a holy and fashionable awe—seldom agree with the person in the street; some smile tolerantly at them, others turn their backs. Yet this ridiculed person, who claims to know nothing about art, who only knows what they like, is a person of the utmost worth. Their opinion deserves recognition because culture is never the product of only a special few. They will be the first to admit to being a mere child in the school of 'isms; but blessed are all 'people on the street' for they truly are the kingdom of art. I am proud to be a member of that group."

I too am proud to be a member of that group. The Lord loves us so much; that's why he made so many of us.

This book won't try to teach you how to paint but rather what to paint, and how to sell it, in order to succeed (and grow) as an artist in your own small town or rural area. I'll tell you what I've done and why. It may not work for everyone, but it works for me.

Mike's House,
15x22 inches,
watercolor.

MEET THE ARTIST

Since the thrust of this book is directed to you, Joe and JoAnn Average, it might be appropriate to let you know the author too is Joe Average wanting to share information with artists in situations similar to his. Having spent most of his life in the small village of Hamburg, Pennsylvania, Stewart Biehl devoted the majority of his time until his retirement a few years ago to furthering his career and helping his wife, Grace, raise their two daughters. Only since then has he been able to spend much time on his art, but he has used that time to develop methods that allow him to operate sucessfully as an artist in his hometown. Here's a brief interview with Stewart to let you get to know him better.

Q. Were you interested in art as a child?

I did not constantly draw pictures as a youngster (although I do now), and our school system did not have art courses at that time, in either the elementary or secondary level. My background as a young man was not an artistic one, but rather a mechanical one.

Q. Did you have any formal art training?

Following high school I graduated from the Wyomissing Polytechnic Institute with a degree in engineering technology and put this knowledge to good use while serving in the U.S. Navy during World War II. A major portion of this time was spent at sea. When I got back to civilian life, I completed my education at Penn State in the field of marketing and merchandising.

Q. How did this background help you in your art career?

Strange as it may seem, an engineering background is extremely helpful to someone who paints in watercolors. In engineering you learn to think and plan in an orderly fashion. Executing good watercolors requires a great deal of planning. Engineering also provides training on the draftsman's drawing board. This background helped me to make architectural drawings fairly easily.

The final test for a painting is the acceptance and approval of the ultimate critic—the customer. The collage painting I did for Mrs. Flickinger is not a masterpiece (see page 58), but it included many beloved details of her home. Her letter shows how she felt about it, and that's good enough for me.

Q. And then what did you do?

For seventeen years I owned and operated Biehl's Stationery and PhotoSupply Co. in Hamburg. In 1967 I sold the business to become the business manager/treasurer of the newly formed Hamburg Area School District, a merger of seven small districts into one large district. This business background was completely alien to a desire to express myself artistically, but the photographic experiences were extremely helpful once I started to paint.

Dear Stu,   Jan 10, 1989
    Now you've done it—you've really done it! And as the expression goes—you've outdone yourself! Can you tell how tremendous I feel the collage is? Everyone that has seen it appreciates the fine detail, the fine art, the perfect positioning of the objects.
    Thank you for giving me many hours of enjoyment, many hours of pleasure in owning this picture.
        Sincerely,
        Carolyn Flickinger

Q. How did you get started painting?

In the fifties I was seeking a more relaxing outlet or hobby and I was attracted to painting in oils. I bought several "how to" art books (this was the start of my library), and attended a group class locally for six sessions. From that point on it was a matter of working by myself—trial and error—solving problems by myself. I liked it and became fairly proficient as a weekend painter. But, as I think back to that period, I never had the same enthusiasm for oils as I had when I discovered watercolors.

Q. When did you get involved in watercolors?

In 1960 I became friendly with Phil Costigan, a New York illustrator and fine artist who retired to our area. Phil was an excellent painter, teacher, and friend who introduced me to watercolors. His close buddy in New York was Ted Kautzky and he never tired of telling stories about Kautzky to the point that I felt that I knew him too. Unfortunately, I never got to know him, since Kautzky died in 1953, but he lives on in my heart through his books and Phil's stories.

Q. Why do you like to paint?

For many years I used to find great enjoyment and relaxation in playing golf. Now I experience those same two elements when painting watercolors. Golf and painting are very similar—this statement usually raises eyebrows, so let me explain. When painting a watercolor you are usually in very pleasant surroundings, and so it is in golf (although sometimes we were crazy enough to play in the rain). You and *you alone* are responsible for the results, a good painting or a good round of golf—it's not a team effort. You can do it alone. Sometimes an expletive is muttered when you make a poorly planned or dumb stroke on your paper; you might hear that same naughty word on the golf course for the same reasons (dumb moves and poor strokes). No two paintings or rounds are the same; you are constantly faced with new challenges. Both activities are relaxing and exciting—relaxing because of the new environment, and exciting when the watercolor washes begin to create a thing of beauty. As a golfer the excitement mounts as you are finishing a great "back nine" after having completed a perfect "front nine."

U.S.S. Ajax, San Diego,
21 x 29 inches,
watercolor.
Collection of the artist.

I served on the U.S.S. Ajax when it was commissioned in San Pedro in 1943. It is berthed in San Diego and I sketched and painted it in 1983 on one of our visits to the West Coast. These trips were made possible by painting and selling some of the things that other artists do not care to do, such as house portraits. That's another reason to pursue success in your small town—every painting you sell supports the habit.

There are, however, two distinct rewards to painting that many other activities do not generate. First, the painting you create expresses a special mood, or re-creates a scene that no longer exists, or evokes a favorable response. This brings you much personal satisfaction. In addition, when that painting is hung for all to see, you provide beauty and enjoyment that is shared by all who view it…again and again.

Second, the income helps. As you begin to sell some of your paintings (and you will), the income—no matter how small at the beginning—helps to support the habit. I don't make a living from my artwork. I could, I'm sure, but I am already retired and don't want to work that hard anymore. However I sell quite a bit of my work, enough to support the habit, enough to travel when my wife and I feel like it, enough to keep enhancing my library, splurge on supplies... all this eases the budget.

Those things, taken together, are more than enough motivation to continue.

Q. How have you succeeded in a small town when you're just "Joe Average"?

When I retired in 1982, I said, "Now I'm going to paint,"—no, let me correct that—"I'm going to *work* at my watercolor and I'm going to become pretty good or pretty frustrated." I'm still not a great artist, or even a very good one, but I'm getting better as I continue to work at it and want to improve even more.

When I started out, I could turn out a fair landscape or view from my imagination. People would like it, but they wouldn't buy it. So I started to paint familiar scenes around town, such as the back alleys, the churches, the industries, the back lots of the foundries, some of the older homes that looked interesting—pieces that I liked, that might be dramatic, and that *I wanted to do*. I began displaying these paintings in the window of a local bank and sold quite a few. Then people began asking me to paint special things for them. Before long, I was making enough from my painting to pay for the supplies and still give me a little pocket change.

I guess I stumbled onto one of the secrets of succeeding in a small town—painting subjects that have a local connection. That's not hard to do, because there are plenty of subjects in a small town that challenge one's artistic talent. And it's something any artist can do, no matter what your style or medium.

The other secret is how you define success. If your goal is to get rich or famous, you may need to follow a path that's different from mine. But if you want to enjoy your painting, add a measure of enjoyment to your friends' and neighbors' lives, and make a little money in the process, you *can* succeed as an artist in your own hometown.

Violin and Bow,
20 x 24 inches,
oil.

I did this painting in oil thirty years ago. I enjoyed doing oils, but once I was introduced to watercolors by my friend Phil Costigan I never returned to oils. My interest in music didn't fade away, but I did make a switch from violin to viola.

CHAPTER 1

What you need to paint

■ Ninety percent of the books published to date are directed toward encouraging the novice to get started, helping the intermediate painter improve, and in some instances refining the skills of the professional. These books discuss at some length the materials you need to paint, so I'm assuming you already have been exposed to these presentations and don't need them repeated here. If you've been painting for a while you no doubt know what materials work best for you—by all means continue to use them. There is no magic in materials or equipment—they don't paint, you do! But some of you may be wondering what I use, so I'll present a summary here of what works for me and why. I won't try to tell you everything about what to buy, just the things that are unique about the way I work.

PAPER

Like most painters I experimented with all the papers available in most weights, contents, and grades until I became confused. Finally I decided to eliminate some of the variables and settle for one paper until I had all other elements under control; then I could return to experiment in this area. I buy Arches 140-pound cold press, Imperial size, and do 75 percent of my work on half sheets, 15x22 inches. The other 25 percent is done on full sheets, 22x30 inches. I now use 300-pound paper for some projects but my favorite is still 140-pound Arches CP 22x30 inches, which I cut to half and quarter sheets as needed. There are many excellent 100 percent rag papers available in varying weights — Arches, Whatman Fabriano,

Waterford, Strathmore, Gemini, and so on.

I used to buy paper ten sheets at a time. But after I started to sell some of my work, I started buying paper in quire lots (25 sheets) and now in four-quire (100 sheet) lots because it lowers the net price per sheet drastically.

There is also a psychological benefit to consider. When a novice starts to paint, that expensive single sheet of white paper is intimidating and the painter proceeds with caution. Boy, was I cautious! But when there was a larger stack of paper on hand I began to relax a bit, knowing that if I made errors it didn't matter because there was an ample supply still available in the stock room. It loosened me up quite a bit.

Raccoon
Shangri La,
24 x 18 inches,
watercolor.

While walking in our park by the Schuylkill River I discovered this tree that was invaded by a family of raccoons. They slept in the daytime while I sketched and painted. I developed my palette of twelve tube colors by trial and error—for this painting, I used raw sienna, cadmium orange, burnt sienna, alizarin crimson, and French ultramarine.

BRUSHES

Here is where you need to heed the advice of the old pros —buy the best brushes you can afford. When I started I was sure that a brush is a brush is a brush. Not so! It took me a long time to realize that a good sable brush lasts longer than the blends. Thirty years ago I bought several low price blends and one ½-inch flat sable. I paid $25 for that sable brush thirty years ago and *I am still using it!* The blends are long gone.

I currently use the usual assortment: three round sables, 5, 8, and 14; three aquarelle flats, ½, ¾, and 1 inch; two flat sables, ½ and 1¼ inch; a 2-inch skywash; and a no. 3 rigger. In addition, there is a miscellaneous group of special brushes I use on occasion: bristles for scrubbing and lifting, and snipped and trimmed worn-out brushes for weeds and texture.

PALETTE

There are many good palettes available and if you're like me you probably have used several. I currently use the Zoltan Szabo palette (which is sold by his company) because it has sixteen color wells and I use twelve tube colors. This leaves four extra wells for additional colors and I use the extras in this fashion: First, I use two wells for cadmium yellow and two wells for burnt sienna. Why two? I like to mix my greens, so that means I go into the yellow well quite frequently and after a bit that yellow becomes contaminated. When I want a pure, clean yellow I use the second well.

The same principle applies to burnt sienna. I use the sienna as a great mixer for some of the darker greens and interesting grays. All of this activity pollutes the first well, so I reserve the second one for those times when I need a clean burnt sienna. In addition to sixteen color wells the Szabo palette has six large wells for making the large color pools you need for washes and glazes. An even larger mixing area is provided in the lid.

COLORS

Several of the books I've suggested in the Bibliography have huge sections devoted to palette colors and color theory, so discussing those topics here would be redundant. I developed my palette by trial and error; it is composed of what I think is the best of three workshop teachers' recommendations:

- Alizarin Crimson
- Winsor Green
- Cadmium Red
- Cerulean Blue
- Burnt Sienna
- Winsor Blue
- Cadmium Orange
- French Ultramarine
- New Gamboge
- Indigo
- Cadmium Yellow
- Raw Sienna

Like all painters I sometimes develop muddy colors. Here again I found that eliminating some of the variables helped. I discovered the problem was that I was too heavy-handed with the browns when producing my darks. When I eliminated burnt umber from my palette most of the mud disappeared. Some time in the future I'll add it to the palette again and hopefully when I do, I'll be able to use it properly.

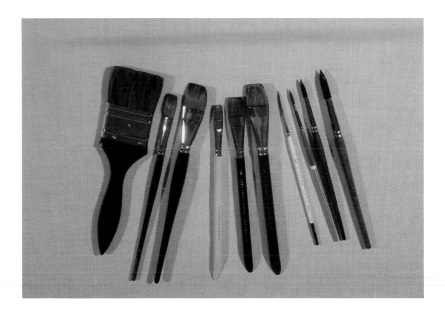

Use the best brushes you can afford—this is one item where you really do get what you pay for. I use (from left) a 2-inch skywash; ½-inch and 1¼-inch flat sables; ½-inch, ¾-inch, and 1-inch aquarelle flats; no. 3 rigger; and nos. 5, 8, and 14 round sables.

EASEL

Outdoor folding easels are varied and in some instances quite expensive. I would suggest moving slowly in this area. You'll soon learn what would be handy and what you need. I bought a French easel some years ago for work outdoors, because I saw so many of them. However, as time went on I developed a way to mount a working surface on a sturdy photographer's tripod. It is lighter and easier to carry about. Had I waited a bit I would have saved some money by not buying the French easel.

I like to carry my gear in a heavy canvas tote bag and prefer it to a wooden box such as a French easel. I already had a sturdy photographer's tripod (and I emphasize the word *sturdy*). For a work surface I purchased a piece of 1/8-inch Masonite and cut it to 24x23 inches; on it I can lay a half sheet (15x22) and still have nine inches left over on which to put my eight-inch wide palette and a small container of water. On the 24-inch side (and 1½ inches from the edge), I cut a hand groove or hand hold 1x4 inches so I could carry it like a suitcase. On the bottom side I mounted an aluminum plate 3x6x¼ inches thick in the center of the 24x23-inch area. In the exact center of the plate I drilled and tapped a hole the same size and number of threads as the screw that holds my camera on the tripod. Then I mounted that work surface on the tripod; it can be tilted and swiveled to any angle and position. Admittedly, this surface cannot be leaned on or subjected to a lot of weight, but it does provide an acceptable lightweight work surface.

Trash Burner,
14½ x 21½ inches,
watercolor.
Collection of the artist.

This was the first painting I did using a newly purchased French easel. I later regretted purchasing the easel, because I developed an easel that suits my purposes better using a photographer's tripod. This location is a few miles south of our town, and the painting is one of the few watercolors I did "as it was"—without rearranging the natural scene.

MISCELLANEOUS SUPPLIES

Sketchbooks

I prefer the spiral-bound kind so the book will lie flat — sometimes you sketch on both sheets if you have a long horizontal format. Or you may want to fold the book in half when holding the book for a sketch. Hard-bound books don't have this flexibility.

A large variety of sketchbooks is available with a hundred different weights and grades of paper. I prefer the books that contain heavyweight rag bond paper, at least 70 pounds or more. When you make a pencil or ink-line sketch most any paper will do, but most of the time I will make a simple watercolor wash sketch and then that 70-pound rag bond will make a nicer, neater sketch because it is so receptive to water.

This is the first sketch I made in preparation for the painting opposite page one. It was done from the front seat of my car using a spiral-bound sketchbook. It is very rough and tentative, but the written notes helped me to recall the scene in vivid detail.

If I've done a pencil sketch, but want more clarification than a pencil value sketch will provide, I lay a page from a second book over the pencil sketch, trace it, and then make a preliminary color sketch with the two books side by side. This is another reason why I prefer spiral-bound books instead of the inflexible hard-bound books. Sometimes I lay my spiral sketchbooks flat and make two sketches of the same subject side by side, one on each side of the spiral. Back in the studio, I've even done this with two sketchbooks flat; this provides four pages for the same subject—one sketch in pencil and one in sepia watercolor, and two different color quickies. This way I can compare all four sketches at one time instead of flipping the pages back and forth.

A word of caution: You must be careful not to get too involved in detailed sketching or you'll soon be spending more time on them than on the watercolor itself. I like to make sketches; I like to attempt to solve all the problems at that level—that is my style. Some painters use only very loose sketches and proceed from there. I urge you to do what works best for you.

Masking Fluid

Some artists never use masking fluid and some use it sparingly. It took me a long time to learn how to use it. It can be thinned with water, which makes it so much easier to apply. I used to apply it with an old brush and had a hard time getting fine lines and sharp corners. Then I learned that you can lay down fine lines by using a dip pen, and you can get square corners using the broad lettering pens. You'll find many uses for it.

I've discovered another product that has been put on the market recently that is helpful for applying masking fluid. It is called The Incredible Nib and is offered by Jerry Griffith Art Products (10833 Farragut Hills Blvd., Knoxville, TN, 37922). It has a wide variety of uses — use it as a brush to apply paint or remove paint — but I mention it here because with it you can apply masking fluid in straight lines, and obtain sharp corners and angles.

Sometimes I make several different sketches of the same scene, as shown here. The first sketch is done in pencil only, while the second uses a touch of color. Both are valuable references when I get back to the studio and begin painting.

Pencils and Erasers
I find that no. 2B pencils are fine for simple value sketches, along with the broad-nosed carpenter's pencils for filling in large dark areas. The Pink Pearl and art gum erasers are adequate, but the kneaded art erasers are best.

Sponges
I use a large cellulose sponge to touch my brushes onto to remove excess water both before and after picking up pigment. Several small two-inch and three-inch natural elephant ear sponges are handy for removing paint from paper or applying texture to the paper. You'll find many uses for them.

Scraping Tools
Brush handles, credit card edges, razors, pocket knives, fingernails—they are all used to scrape pigment on a drying wash to create interesting textures and shapes. Keep plenty of these odds and ends handy.

Hair Dryer
In the studio this is a real time-saver. That hot blast of air will speed the drying of the whole painting or just a selected area.

Water Spray Bottles
Most hardware stores have them. They're useful to apply water to the whole sheet or just isolated sections and helpful to keep the pigments moist in your palette.

Mail-order Catalogs
You won't use these to paint but you will use them to learn what kind of art supplies are available. These companies advertise in art magazines and I urge you to build a collection of catalogs from the bigger mail-order houses. There are about eight to ten good ones. If you live close to a good supply house (within reasonable commuting distance) you won't need the catalogs except to compare prices. But if you don't live in a major market area, you'll need the catalogs .

Drawing Board

I've tried them all—plywood and Masonite treated with varnish, Lucite and Formica with clamps on the corners, watercolor blocks with clamps, drawing boards with gummed tape.

I prefer to mount my paper onto Homosote board. This is a soft building material with properties very similar to cork board but it is more durable and cheaper.

I'm sure your local building supply house has Homosote board in stock. Mine has it in sheet size 24x48 inches and ½-inch thick.

Initially I purchased two Homosote boards and took them to a local carpenter/cabinet shop and had them cut the boards to the sizes as illustrated on the diagrams. This gave me a total of six surfaces upon which to mount paper.

Since I've been using this system I've purchased more 24x48-inch boards so I now have a large supply of boards to accommodate quarter, half, and full sheets. This way I can have a ready supply of mounted paper available in all three sizes.

I staple paper onto Homosote board to create drawing boards. It's durable, inexpensive, and accepts staples or tacks much more easily than plywood. I bought two sheets of Homosote from the building supply house and had them cut as shown to provide six drawing surfaces of varying sizes.

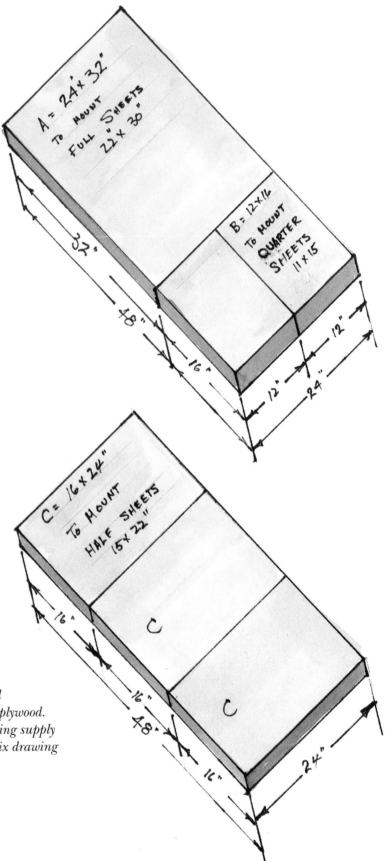

STRETCHING THE PAPER

There are many ways to treat the painting surface. You can use watercolor blocks; four corner clamps and board; thumbtacks on board; or gummed tape on drawing board. The method I use is a bit different. I use staples on Homosote board to mount my 140-pound or even 300-pound paper for a perfect watercolor surface.

The mounting procedure is simple. We have a laundry tub large enough to soak quarter and half sheets in several inches of tap water (do not use hot water). Immerse the paper for approximately ten to fifteen minutes, until it expands fully. Lift the paper by one edge and let the water flow off the surface until it doesn't drip anymore.

Now lay it on your board and staple the four edges to the board with a staple gun, placing a staple every three inches. You can use a desktop stapler but I opted to purchase an inexpensive gun tacker and use light-duty ⁵⁄₁₆-inch wire staples. Place your staples ⅛ inch from the edge. If the staples do not fully penetrate the board, take an old table knife or similar flat instrument and use the flat side to push the staple fully into the board.

Now you're finished. Lay the board flat on the floor and let the paper dry. If you need a quick dry, you can lay it flat in the sun and it will dry fairly fast. Faster still, use a hair dryer. I generally let my pieces dry overnight.

When the paper dries it will be *smooth and flat* with nary a buckle. In fact, look at the staples and you will see how the paper has contracted as it dried. The dry paper will be tight as a drum.

I usually sketch my design or subject onto the paper *before* I mount it; not a complete detailed drawing, but rather the large shapes. Soaking or stretching the paper will not affect the drawing. After the paper is mounted and dried you can continue the drawing to its completion and include as little or as much detail as your style warrants. Personally, I prefer to have my drawings fairly complete before I start to paint. I don't want to make drawing decisions while I am painting. Then I can concentrate on the other variables, such as value and color.

CHAPTER 2

*I*n the studio

We all wish for and dream about creating the ideal studio, one that will be spacious, functional, beautiful, and the envy of all who see it. Studios, however, like fancy supplies, do not create exciting paintings… you do! Yes, it helps if you are able to work in perfect surroundings, but not much. The end result is still up to you!

So don't worry if you don't have the money or space to create your dream studio. This chapter will give you some ideas about how to set up or redo your studio so it's both inexpensive and effective, plus ideas for some simple items you can make and use in your studio that will help achieve professional results.

SETTING UP A STUDIO

Where to paint in your home is going to depend on many factors: the spaces you have available, your family size, and your finances. Many of us have started at the same place—the kitchen table—and branched out from there. After our children grew up, graduated from college, and moved on with their lives, our nest became empty enough that I was able to take over two bedrooms and convert them to studio space. Some artists are able to develop studio space in their basement, possibly an attic, or even the garage.

Whether you're setting up your first studio or redoing an old one, keep in mind that design help is available. From time to time the art magazines will print special reports on creating space for a studio and even show several examples of areas some artists have created for themselves. Reprints of these articles are available by contacting the magazine.

Two Suggestions
First, I would (and did) proceed very slowly and carefully in developing a working space. Remodeling an area in your home, be it bedroom, basement, addition, or garage, can be costly and when one is in the embryo stage it is most important to get the biggest bang for your buck…you don't want to do it too often. This also applies to furniture; s*imple is better!* The beautiful pieces of drawing furniture and drawing files are nice, but they are expensive, so a good deal of research is imperative.

The second suggestion is to plan your space for "leave it lay" convenience. One of the problems of painting in a space used for many purposes, such as the kitchen table, the dining room table, or a temporary table in the family room, is that you must get all your material out of its storage space in the closet and when finished, return it all back to the closet. That doesn't give you the luxury of stopping for

Birch Tree by the Shop,
10½ x 14½ inches,
watercolor.
Collection of the artist.

I urge you to proceed slowly and carefully when developing a permanent working space. This outbuilding alongside the big birch is in our backyard and my first inclination was to convert it into a permanent studio. But it was a raw building that had no insulation, no heat, and no water, and was just 10x15 feet. It would have been a great showplace, decorated just right, and private, too, but too costly to convert. I opted to take over two bedrooms on our third floor instead. That turned out to be less expensive and even more private because visitors can't just drop in as they please. So analyze your situation and make decisions to fit what is available to you.

an hour or two for lunch, or a quick trip uptown or whatever. This special convenience is what I mean; the freedom to walk away and leave it lay.

If a corner of one room is all you can have at the moment, opt for the corner of a bedroom. You only use it a third of the twenty-four-hour day and even then you don't see the condition of the room because you are asleep. In addition, visitors don't go trooping through it several times a day. It is a *private place* so when you want to interrupt your painting you can leave your spread "as is" until you choose to return to it. A small portable screen will shield the whole corner for longer periods if you want even more privacy.

Lighting

You can light your watercolor board very easily in several ways. You can use a fluorescent shop-type fixture using two four-foot, 40 watt tubes, one cool white and one daylight. Combine this with a 75-watt incandescent bulb to provide a balance of warm light. If this isn't practical, then use a flexible combo lamp that has a circleline fluorescent tube in conjunction with an incandescent bulb.

OTHER STUDIO HELPS

You are a creative person (or you wouldn't be painting) and many simple devices or ideas will come to you that will help you paint and will help make the process a little easier. Here are a few of mine. I'm sure you'll come up with many more.

Slide Viewers

I use a slide viewer quite a bit in my studio. Quite frequently slides of a subject area are all I have and it is from these that I will develop working sketches from which to paint. Even when my sketches are developed at the site, I still take a series of slides of the subject and refer to them for detail while painting in the studio.

Many artists have older slide viewers that don't have a fan, which can damage slides left in the viewer for a long time and shorten the life of the bulb. For example, I use the Simon SVS5822 slide viewer. It has a viewing screen size that is 8x8 inches and also has 3x and 22x magnification. It is a good viewer but it doesn't have a bulb cooling fan. The models now do have a fan but what do you do with the older model?

I devised this "Rube Goldberg" cooling fan and I'm happy to report it works well. I can leave a slide in the viewer for extended periods of time and it is not affected by heat and the life of the bulb has been prolonged. You may have some other type of viewer that could use some auxiliary cooling air. Perhaps the sketch at right will help to get your ideas flowing so you can create your own cooling system.

If you use a slide projector, you may have experienced early bulb burn-outs. The main reason for this is excess heat. Most all of the projectors manufactured today have an adequate bulb-cooling system while in use, but many people turn off their projector as soon as they are finished using it. To increase bulb life you must let the fan run for a long time to cool the bulb down to room temperature.

Easy Wipes

All watercolorists need wipes, pick-ups, etc. for quick clean-ups. Tissues do a great job, but there is an inexpensive alternative. I do this: On my shelf above my drawing board I put a roll of toilet tissue in a homemade wooden holder (no elaborate design). I can pull it off quickly for a quick wipe or clean-up.

Like most watercolorists I am plagued by "watercolor mud" on my paintings. It took me a long time to realize that one of the contributors to mud (and there are many) is an unclean palette; clean washes are produced by clean pigment, clean water, clean brushes, and a clean mixing area. The key word here is clean, so I wipe my palette mixing areas after each wash and this quick wipe gadget makes it easier and inexpensive to do.

I also keep a small bowl of prefolded pads on that same shelf—a plastic butter or margarine tub does nicely to hold them. I fold toilet paper into a number of pads about two inches square; they are easy to grab and make a quick blot of a mistake or an unwanted drop or drip. When I paint, I usually have a paper pad in my left hand. It is great for blotting excess water off the heel of a brush or for dabbing a newly painted edge to make parts of that edge lost and found. That little pad is great for making a quick blot when the value of the first touch of the brush is too strong.

Nothing too spectacular, but it works for me.

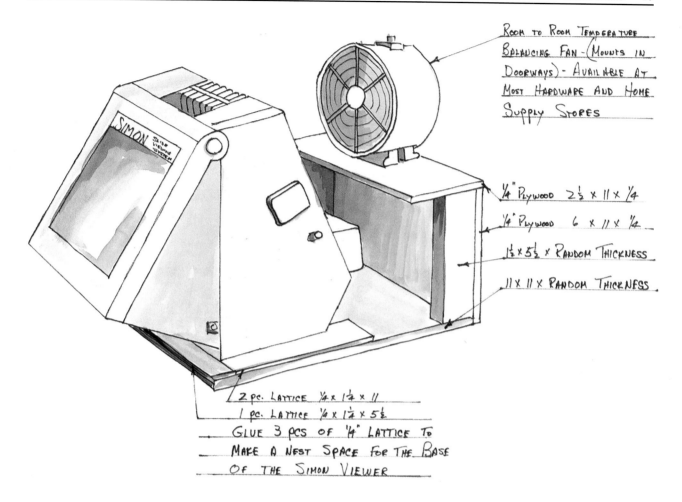

ROOM TO ROOM TEMPERATURE
BALANCING FAN - (MOUNTS IN
DOORWAYS) - AVAILABLE AT
MOST HARDWARE AND HOME
SUPPLY STORES

1/4" PLYWOOD 2 1/2 × 11 × 1/4
1/4" PLYWOOD 6 × 11 × 1/4
1 1/2 × 5 1/2 × RANDOM THICKNESS
11 × 11 × RANDOM THICKNESS

2 PC. LATTICE 1/4 × 1 1/4 × 11
1 PC. LATTICE 1/4 × 1 1/4 × 5 1/2
GLUE 3 PCS OF 1/4" LATTICE TO
MAKE A NEST SPACE FOR THE BASE
OF THE SIMON VIEWER

You can stretch your art budget by coming up with ways to build or modify your equipment to suit your needs. Here's how I added a cooling fan to my slide viewer so I can view reference slides for a long time without worrying about damage by the heat.

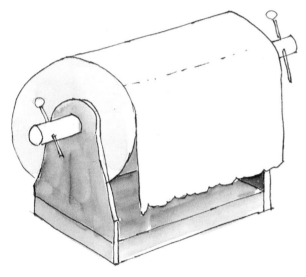

I made a simple wooden holder like this one to hold a roll of toilet paper and put it on a shelf above my drawing board, so now I always have wipes close by for quick clean-ups. It's handy and saves me a few pennies over the cost of a box of tissues.

Leaning Bridge

I enjoy painting architectural subjects (I call them architectural landscapes) and sometimes attention to detail is required. A transparent artist's leaning bridge is very helpful. It allows you to see your work at all times while keeping your hands clean and your work smudge free; you lean your hand on the bridge and not your painting while doing detail work. Bridges are available from most art supply houses in varying lengths from twelve to twenty-four inches, and cost $15 to $20.

If your budget doesn't permit buying a transparent bridge you can make a simple device I call a ruling bridge. It may not be transparent but it will help you when you paint details because the leaning feature is the most important one. It will also serve as a straightedge when painting lines with brush or pen and as a handy measuring rule for use in the field. Here's how to make one: Take a yardstick and cut it at the twenty-two-inch line. Next cut off a two-inch section, cutting at the twenty-inch line. Then cut another two inches off at the eighteen-inch line. Glue one two-inch pad underneath each end and now you have an eighteen-inch ruling bridge that you can use in your studio and in your outdoor painting and sketching kit.

When painting lines, don't place the brush against the rule. Instead, as illustrated in the sketch, hold the brush with your thumb and index finger and have the remaining fingers slide along the edge. The line you draw can be varied thick to thin, rough to smooth by varying the pressure of the fingers holding the brush.

A transparent leaning bridge gives you a place to rest your hand so that you don't smudge your work, but still allows you to see the painting.

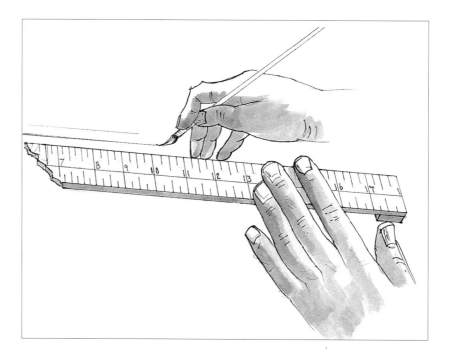

A homemade ruling bridge is less expensive than a leaning bridge and also prevents smudging. You can't see through it, but you can use it as a straightedge.

TRANSFERRING SMALL DRAWINGS TO THE WORK SURFACE

I've found a method that saves me from a lot of frustration and mistakes in making the drawings for my watercolors. Here's how it came about.

After painting for some time, I reached the conclusion that many landscapes, street scenes, etc., should have some form of life in them. So now I try to include a figure or two—sometimes a dog or cat, maybe a flock of birds or geese, but mostly people.

But this created a problem. I try to do as little erasing as possible on the watercolor sheet because I don't want to damage the surface, but I found I had to make quite a few erasures when drawing people because I'm not the world's fastest or most accomplished drawer of figures. (Everett Draper's two books listed in the Bibliography have been very helpful along these lines.)

I solved the problem by drawing figures on a separate piece of paper and transferring them to the watercolor paper. This allows me to make all the changes in the figures I want without worrying about erasure damage.

I usually decide where to insert a figure after the rest of the preliminary drawing is finished. I do this by putting a small piece of tracing paper over the approximate spot and making a few quick figure drawings (stick figures will do) to determine the size.

Once this is determined, the actual drawing is made on another clean piece of paper rather than on the finished drawing. When the figure is completed, transfer it to the watercolor paper:

I like to draw some parts of the scene, such as figures, on a separate piece of paper and transfer them to the drawing surface. This allows me to experiment freely and keeps me from damaging the paper by too much erasure. When I've drawn the figure to my liking, the first step is to transfer the drawing to tracing paper. Then I turn the tracing paper over and retrace the lines from the back. Next I turn the tracing paper back over, position it on the drawing surface, and use the back of a spoon to transfer the drawing to the paper.

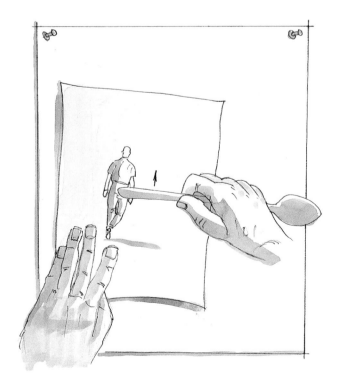

1. Put a small piece of tracing paper over the drawing of the figure and, using a sharp, soft pencil (no. 2B or softer), trace your drawing. I emphasize *sharp—make it needle sharp.*

2. Flip your tracing paper over and run your sharp pencil over lines you just made.

3. Turn your tracing paper back over and place it on the spot on the watercolor paper where you want the figure to appear. Holding the tracing paper down firmly with your left hand and using the blunt side of a spoon handle, rub the figure as shown in the sketch. Your figure will transfer neatly. Now all you have to do is clean up or strengthen the lines as much as you need to for your painting.

You can use this same method to transfer any drawing—figures, animals, flowers, or small item that you may want to draw separately. But save this method for small elements. If the separate drawings get too large, the system becomes rather tedious.

Trial Mats

When I've finished a painting, I like to spend some time looking at it to see if it's *really* finished. Many times I'll prop it up against the wall or furniture opposite my favorite relaxing chair (usually next to the telly). I look at it from time to time and ask myself:

- Does it carry across the room?
- Are the values correct?
- Did I miss something?

I like to view the painting in a mat so I get a sense of how the painting will look when framed. I use something I call my trial mat sandwich to do this. The sandwich lets me prop up the painting in a mat anywhere I like, even move it from place to place. I use two types, one for a painting still mounted on the Homosote board and one for a painting that's already been removed.

Here's how I make a trial mat sandwich for a painting that hasn't been removed from the board:

1. I use mats that are 22x28 inches, so I have a piece of ¼-inch plywood cut to 22x28 inches. I then center a Homosote board on the piece of plywood and establish a line for the bottom positioning of the board that allows the watercolor to show through the 14x20-inch mat opening.

2. Then I glue two pieces of 1x28-inch lattice along that line. This lattice provides a shelf upon which the drawing board can sit. Lattice strips are available at your local lumber yard and are ¼-inch thick. I glue one on top of the other to make a ½-inch shelf for the mounting board to rest on.

3. I set my mounting board on the lattice shelf and place a mat on top, and the trial mat sandwich is complete. I can prop it against a wall and see how the painting looks.

Sometimes I have removed the staples and the watercolor from the drawing board and I still want to see the painting in a trial mat. For this I use a thinner trial mat sandwich. Here's how to make one:

1. Take a piece of mat board (or any other piece of stiff material such as chip board or corrugated board) and trim it to the size of the trial mat. Lay the trial mat on it and draw the mat opening onto the board.

2. Now draw a 45-degree line across the bottom corners as in the diagram and cut this slit with a craft knife.

3. Slip the bottom corners of the painting into the slits, place the mat on top, clip the sandwich together with a spring clamp, and your thin trial mat sandwich is complete. You can place this sandwich most anywhere and study the watercolor at your leisure.

It's a good idea to spend time looking at a finished painting to see if it needs any changes. I put the painting in a trial mat so I can see what it will look like once it's framed. I use a piece of plywood board with a ledge that the painting sits on and a standard size mat.

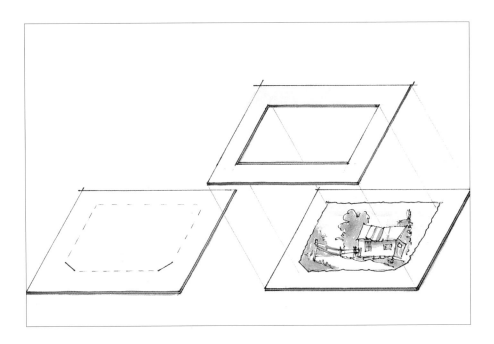

When I want to view a painting that's been taken off the drawing board, I use a piece of mat board with slits in the corners. I can slide the painting into the slits and put a mat on top, clip the pieces together, and prop it up anywhere in the room.

Light Boxes

Has this happened to you? You've planned a painting that requires a fairly accurate and detailed drawing. In the middle of the painting (or even close to completion) you've made a mistake in value, or design, or had some sloppy handling that cannot be corrected, so you're faced with the prospect of starting all over again. I used to get so discouraged that most of the time I just set the whole project aside. There had to be some way to ease that shock and pain.

I came to the conclusion that a light box/slide viewer would be helpful at a time like this. It would allow me to trace the drawing of the ruined painting onto a clean sheet of paper, saving me the frustration of having to redraw the scene, and would be useful for other purposes as well. There are a number of commercial tracing boxes available, but I needed one that would accommodate half sheets (15x22 inches) and they were too costly for my budget. Second, the lights in the box had to be strong enough to allow me to trace through 140-pound watercolor paper and the light boxes available didn't provide that much light. So I decided to design my own; the results are illustrated in the sketch below.

Does it work? Yes indeed it does; in fact I've found many other uses for the light box over and above the original intent:

1. Tracing through a ruined 140-pound watercolor to a new 140-pound sheet. The lights are strong enough that you can easily transfer the images. You can also trace images through 300-pound sheets. You will not be able to trace all the details but certainly the larger images will come through. Naturally once the image is transferred you will have to sharpen up some lines and areas, but at least you do not have to start from the very beginning with an empty sheet.

2. Sorting slides. The glass surface is large enough that you can put a large number of slides on it for viewing, sorting, rearranging, and editing.

3. Sorting negatives. Lay your photographic negatives on the ground glass for recording and sorting.

4. Tracing preliminary sketches. I usually make a small preliminary value sketch before I begin an important watercolor. The first sketch is usually in black values. I can trace that original sketch many times over and experiment with color values, knowing that if I make a mistake or want to see yet another combination it is easy to duplicate that first careful drawing.

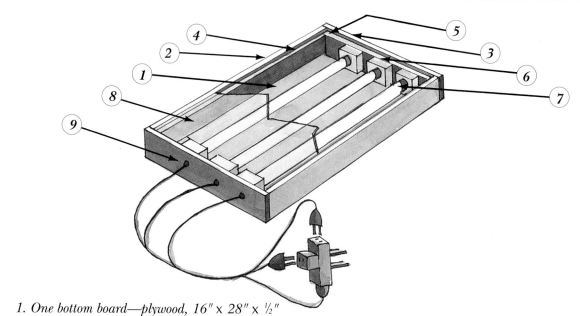

1. *One bottom board—plywood, 16" x 28" x ½"*
   covered with aluminum foil for reflection
2. *Two side pieces—plywood, 3½" x 28" x ¾"*
3. *Two end pieces—plywood, 3½" x 17½" x ¾"*
4. *Tack lattice to side and end pieces to support*
   frosted glass top. Side lattices—
   1¼" x ¼" x 28"
5. *End lattices—1¼" x ¼" x 17½"*
6. *Space three or four fluorescent fixtures evenly*
7. *Use 24", 20-watt white fluorescent tubes*
8. *Sheet of frosted glass from local glazier, 16" x 28"*
9. *Drill three holes in side for light fixture cords*

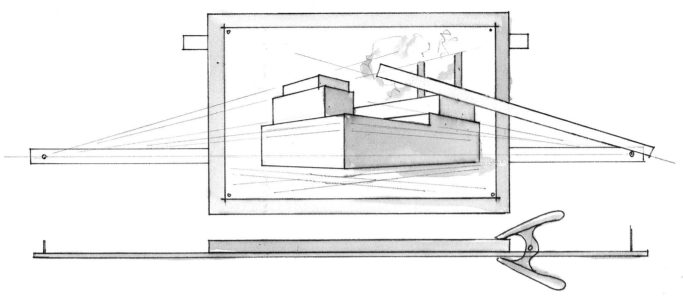

I used lattice strips to construct this easy-to-use perspective guide. I place the drawing board on two strips of lattice. The bottom lattice strip lines up with the eye-level line and the nail with the right vanishing point. Then I put another piece of lattice against the nail and use it as a pivot to establish the perspective lines. As you can see from the side view, I use a clamp to hold the drawing board and lattice together.

Perspective Guide

I have devised a simple device that is helpful when doing watercolors that require fairly accurate perspective in the drawing. In many drawings, the vanishing point is far off to the left or right of the drawing board—sometimes *way* off the board. I purchased lattice strips 1⅛ x ³/₁₆ inches and cut them into three lengths of three, four, and five feet. In one end I drove a nail; this provided me with a pivot point at the vanishing point (VP).

For illustrative purposes, let's assume that the VP will be about three feet to the right of the drawing. Take the four-foot lattice and lay it on your drawing table, with the lattice approximately on the eye-level line and the pivot nail to the right at the approximate VP. Take another lattice strip the approximate length of your drawing board and lay it on the drawing table so that the top of your drawing board will rest on it.

Now lay your drawing board on the top of the two lattice strips so your eye level will line up with the bottom strip. Your board will rest flat on the two lattice strips and will not wobble. When you start to draw, determine exactly where the right VP will be and slide the lattice until the pivot nail is at the VP. Once this is done, I usually place an alligator spring clamp on the drawing board and lattice to prevent it from sliding.

Use one of the remaining lattice strips as a straightedge. Place one edge against the pivot nail (which is now locked in over the VP) and you can then draw all of your perspective lines with ease.

Wagners and
Wengerts Corner,
14½ x 21½ inches,
watercolor.

A scene such as this is much easier to render using a perspective device like the one described here. The lines for the window, roof edges, and siding can be drawn in quickly and easily.

CHAPTER 3

Growing as an artist

■ Interaction with other artists and their work is important to every artist's development. Art societies, workshops, and classes allow you to meet with, paint with, and socialize with other artists. You critique one another's work (respectfully so), you exchange ideas, you discuss materials and techniques, and all this sets the creative mechanism into motion.

But you choose not to live in, or close to, the larger metropolitan areas and do not have easy access to the daily or weekly classes offered by art schools and societies. Or you may not be able to participate because you are not yet ready to devote full time to your art. By and large you work alone, in isolation, either by choice or by circumstances.

So how do you grow? The following ideas (ideas that do work) will help.

BUILD YOUR OWN PERSONAL LIBRARY

Here is one area where more is better. There are many excellent books available by several book clubs and publishers devoted to "how to" and art appreciation.

As an artist, you enjoy looking at and studying the art produced by those you admire. When you buy an artist's book you buy a whole gallery of that artist's work, to enjoy again and again! I'll never be able to buy their originals, but through their books I have a whole shelf full of Ted Kautzky, John Pike, Edgar Whitney, Tony Couch, Zoltan Szabo, Herb Olsen, Tom Hill, LaVere Hutchings, Phil Austin, Ranulph Bye, Eric Sloane, and so many, many more. When I go through a dry spell, and we

all get them from time to time, I peruse my gallery/library— or is it a library/gallery?—and it doesn't take too long for the creative juices to start flowing again.

Books as Teaching Tools
I also use my books as teaching tools. As an example, let's take a book by an artist whose work I admire. Now let's suppose there is a painting in it that I like and it is sort of similar to a future painting stored in my mental computer. I'll use that painting to explore and develop my own idea. Rarely will I emulate the whole painting. Rather, I will break it into sections and see how the artist produced the sky, the weeds, the trees, or the buildings— whatever I admire. Then I switch from a mental process, and physically start a series of simple sketches of my own, and change the angle of the light, vary the colors, alter the mood, and see what develops. Before I know it, I've created my own painting that incorporates a new technique or approach.

The Chapel at Grove City College, 14³/₄ x 21³/₄ inches, watercolor. Collection of Pamela Sue Cranford.

I did this painting as a Christmas surprise for our granddaughter, Pam Sue, so she can remember her days at Grove City College. My several years of painting the "village scene" have given me confidence in my ability to paint this type of subject.

But Books Are So Expensive

What is expensive, $20 to $25? Not really. Look at it this way: If you break out only two or three good ideas or tips, you've done so at the cost of a formal lesson. And really, each book will be good for more than just two or three good ideas—you'll learn many ways to improve your techniques. Also, book clubs make these books available at substantial discounts from retail price.

An Entertainment Bargain

Here is another way to justify a book's cost. Consider the price of a movie today. If you curl up with a good book (turn off the telly) for just two nights, its cost isn't much more than that of going to a couple of movies. Books are an entertainment bargain. What's more, they stay on your shelf forever!

Choosing Your Books

The selection of art books available is so wide that sometimes I wonder how anyone can decide which ones to buy. *Don't let that be a stumbling block*—take advantage of some publisher's thirty-day, no-obligation examination offer. Publishers are constantly improving the descriptive literature about the books they offer

so you as a prospective buyer can make wiser choices. They realize, of course, that there are times when you order a book only to realize it is not quite what you thought it might be. My experience has been that they will accept returns or exchanges quite readily, thus assuring you that you will not have to keep a book that you really don't want.

Choose your authors very carefully by studying at great length the type of work they produce. I always asked myself, "Is this the style I want to emulate; do I really like this artist's work?" Then, too, I make a list of areas and skills that need improvement such as figures, moods, color, perspective, and so on. There are many books devoted entirely to these areas alone.

Using Your Books

I have such a reverence for books and their preservation that it took a long time before I wrote anything in the book itself, not even a margin note. Finally the realization came… hey, these books are mine—to be *used*. Now I pore over them with a highlighter so important areas can be located and emphasized. Marginal notes

are no longer verboten. I do it all the time!

For example, the author may describe the painting procedure in the caption beneath a watercolor. You often wonder which colors the artist used, and the text tells you, but in sentence form rather than in a list form. So now as you read the text and look at the print, your eye flicks back and forth so you soon get lost. I pick the colors out and write them in the margin in *list* form. Now it is so much easier to refer to them when studying the painting and narrative. I underline and highlight all other statements or points I want to recall or refer to.

Supplement the Indexes

Most books have indexes that are very helpful, but I usually supplement them with information of my own. For example, take a subject such as weeds. The index will list the pages where the author describes how to produce weeds and these pages no doubt will also have several pictures. However, if you look at all the other paintings in the book, many of them will have good examples of weeds too, even though the artist's emphasis or

Don't be afraid to really use your books. Here I've supplemented the index of a book by Tony Couch so that I can very quickly put my fingers on additional information that's most helpful to me.

I have a local bindery convert my painting books to spiral-bound so they'll lay flat when open. Then I can leave them lying beside me while I experiment with the suggestions the author makes.

demonstration may be about skies. The index may say, "Foreground-79," and the artist may devote the entire page 79 to explaining his or her thoughts about foregrounds or it may just have one paragraph devoted to it. But if you look at the paintings scattered throughout the book there may be eight or nine illustrations that have effective and innovative foregrounds.

On a separate sheet of paper, I make a list of areas that I am interested in; under each area I list the page number of the illustration that has good examples. My areas usually are:

- buildings/barns
- snow
- utility poles
- fences
- skies
- water
- foregrounds
- trees
- weeds

I tape this page into the index section; seems like a simple procedure, but it sure helps locate illustrations that help.

Accessions List
I strongly urge you to make an accessions list and put it in a simple ring binder. This is a list of additions to your collection of books, your personal library. It should be in two parts: first, a numerical order listing the date you bought the book, plus the title, author, publisher, and the book's cost; second, list the books in alphabetical order, by author and title.

This seems like an unnecessary chore, but as time goes on you tend to forget what books you already have purchased or what books you have loaned to a friend and may have forgotten. The list will help you keep track of your books.

Periodically I spend a "rainy afternoon with my friends"— the books in my personal art library. Occasionally they must be mended, cleaned, and restacked. The last time I did

this, I was surprised to learn that the number of books in my library had reached 212— and it's still growing!

Paperbacks
As I said, I use my books as study vehicles. Many times I will lay a book flat on my table and make a "study print" of a piece or style that I like. Paperbacks do not lie flat, so I take mine to a local printer who trims off the binding and inserts a spiral binding as per the sketch above. The cost is not too great. Many offices also have a machine that punches holes and inserts a plastic binder. Whichever method you use can make your books much more useful.

Jackets
Because you are using books to stimulate and challenge, often your book is at your elbow on the drawing board and vulnerable to the clutter, color drips, water splashes, and the many other things that happen accidentally. Your books need some protection.

Do you remember when you were in school, you were required to make a book wrapper out of brown kraft paper to protect the cover? You also were warned not to write on the inside pages; the book had to be protected because it was going to be passed along to the students in the grades behind you. Even in adult life, I used to wrap my books in brown kraft wrapping paper. Then I learned that I could buy book jackets made of Mylar from library supply companies such as Gaylord—now I can see the colorful prints on the dust covers and also protect those covers from getting torn and ratty from frequent handling.

More is Better

After you've read the previous paragraphs, I think you'll understand what I mean when I say "more is better." This is the one area on which I urge a reader to splurge—become a bit extravagant. I can guarantee that you will return to your library time and time again for help and inspiration, and each time you review a book, you will gain new insights and new motivation.

ATTEND WORKSHOPS BY NATIONALLY KNOWN ARTISTS

Your family responsibilities as well as your personal financial situation will help you decide whether it is possible to attend workshops. They are a very good experience and well worth the time and expense.

A few artists feel intimidated by workshops because they have the notion that many workshops are geared to the advanced, experienced student. Nothing could be further from the truth. Oh sure, every group has a mixture of students from novice to professional but it has been my experience that *all levels help each other*. The demonstrations—watching a painting in progress from start to finish—are a delight and so helpful.

An even larger plus is the camaraderie that develops between participants. The sharing of ideas, the review of a wide variety of paintings, observing and learning how other artists work, meeting other artists in your area—all this is a positive experience.

You don't need to travel far and wide to attend workshops. Study the workshop issues of the two leading art magazines, *The American Artist* and *The Artist's Magazine*, and you'll learn that workshops are held in all areas of this country. I'm positive you can find workshops you would like or prefer to attend within a half day's drive of your home.

Workshops are excellent learning/vacation combinations. My wife, a non-painter, travels with me to all workshops and always enjoys the experience. She manages to pursue her interests in the area either alone or in the company of other non-painters.

Once you have decided to attend, there are a few things to do that will make the experience more meaningful.

Attendance

Try to attend the whole workshop, not just a day or two (though *some* is better than *none*). The instructor many times refers to the previous day's lecture/demonstration and you miss the continuity if you don't attend all of it. In addition, with limited attendance you miss the important interaction with the other students.

Pictures and Notes

Yes indeed—take pictures of the demo in progress, pictures of the subject matter, and even pictures of someone else's interesting painting gear, palette, easel, equipment, whatever.

I usually use a stenographer's note pad for my notes and comments, and I use one per workshop. Now, I don't fill all sixty pages with notes, but I do have pages left over so I can tape some of my snapshots into it.

Unusual Gear

I've seen some participants use the small hand-held mini-tape recorders to record the instructor's comments. Use any device that will help you to recall the moment. I put my small binoculars in my gear bag. I like to watch the demo from the fringes and even though I can see the demo very well, the binoculars help me get that real close look at the work in progress.

Questions

Some novices are timid when it comes to questions; there is no such thing as a "dumb question," so get rid of that timidity. In fact, before I attend a workshop, I use the first few pages of the new steno book I assigned to this upcoming workshop and compile a list of questions I want answers to. These are questions about problems I've encountered or areas where I need help. Most of the time the instructor will answer them during the regular presentation, but if not, I at least have a reminder to ask.

Tony Couch

Tony Couch, watercolorist extraordinaire, is also an excellent teacher and critic whose ideas and techniques are available through workshops, books, and videos to artists working in isolation.

A resident of Stone Mountain, Georgia, Tony is a master at visiting an area, picking out the ordinary and mundane, then using it as subject matter for a colorful and unusual watercolor. He is equally at home painting along the seashore, in the mountains, or in the barnyards of rural America.

Along the coastlines, Tony generally avoids the usual sailboats in the bay and marine scenes portrayed so often. Instead, he haunts the boat repair yards and back bay areas, gets his "imagination wheels" spinning, and watercolors like *Big Sister* are the usual result. (Tony has confided that his marine scenes do sell well—boat owners love them.)

Tony Couch had three simultaneous careers…

watercolor artist, watercolor teacher, and senior pilot for Delta Airlines (he retired in Fall 1989). He fell in love with watercolors when he studied with Edgar A. Whitney at the Pratt Institute in New York City. He has written several books and produced a number of excellent video-tapes and continues to present his popular workshops throughout the United States. (For more information, see the Resources list.)

Big Bite,
by Tony Couch,
22x30 inches,
watercolor.

Workshops by artists such as Tony Couch provide an invaluable opportunity for artists who work in small towns to improve and grow. If your town is too small to have classes by nationally known artists, plan a vacation around a workshop. It's well worth it!

Big Sister,
by Tony Couch,
15x22 inches,
watercolor.

Critiques

Take three or four of your recently completed paintings along. Many instructors will set aside time for a daily critique of the work performed that day. In addition, some will also critique a painting that you brought with you, usually one a day and usually at an evening session. I've heard a lot of students express dismay because they didn't think to bring three or four paintings with them. *Be prepared for this extra bonus!*

Remove the paintings from the frame, let them be matted only. Instructors don't like to handle the frames, glass, et al; besides all that, it will be easier for you to transport them if they are just matted. Of course you must also be prepared to accept and respect those instructors who will only critique the work actually painted during their workshop. If this is the way they work, so be it.

Handling Criticism

The criticism that is generated at workshop critiques is not a personal attack, but rather constructive advice by a respected artist trying to tell you how to improve your paintings. You are paying to attend this artist's workshop so you evidently hold this artist and his or her work in high esteem, therefore it will be to your benefit to take advantage of the criticism. If it pinches a bit, set the hurt aside, because the instructor is only trying to help. Conversely, instructors often offer favorable comments that make you feel ten feet tall.

There are times, however, when your work is criticized by an artist or viewer of lesser status than that professional artist at the workshop. Recognize any criticism of this nature for what it is, poor advice from someone not worthy to render it.

However, all artists, whether growing amateur or accomplished professional, are in need of a friend (crony, chum, buddy, or whatever name you choose), someone who will criticize or review your painting favorably or harshly knowing that you won't banish them to Siberia after they do it. For some reason a trusted crony can spot an obvious oversight or goof at once while you have been painting on and on and missed this same fault. A fresh eye, a new look, seems to be able to do this.

I have a built-in reviewer, an in-house critic, in my wife, who seems to have that uncanny ability to look at a painting and spot "something that just isn't right" and she tells me so. Her biggest complaint is that I don't know when to quit… "stop, it's done!" We don't always agree but I'd venture a guess that she is right and I am wrong about 90 percent of the time.

The ideal situation would be a buddy who is art-trained, but that isn't always possible. But look at it this way, if your artistic ability grows as you continue to work, why can't your in-house critic's ability also develop as you mature? It does!

STUDY VIDEO WORKSHOPS

If you have a VCR (video cassette recorder) you have an unlimited number of workshops available to you right in your own home, workshops by highly respected big-name artists and instructors. The art magazines are full of advertisements featuring home workshops via videos. In addition it is possible to get in-depth studies on specialized subjects (usually one subject per tape) on color, composition, anatomy, perspective, figures, et al.

I have a video done by every artist whose workshop I attended. It is like sitting in the front row of the demo area; if you miss a section, you just stop, rewind, and play it again until you fully understand what was done. These videos along with the book by the artist make a great teaching combination.

The drawback, of course, is that you miss out on the interaction with the instructor and other artists. Videos are like doing portraits from photographs or slides; this may be the only access you have to the subject. Fine. However, the best way to do a portrait is in person…in the round. So it is with videos. Workshops are so much better in person…in the round.

COLLECT VALUE STUDIES

One of the first books I bought for my library was *Painting Trees and Landscapes in Watercolor* by Ted Kautzky. I refer time and time again to pages 8 and 9, which contain his text and accompanying six sketches on value arrangement. This alone was worth the price of the book.

Value studies are the experimental placement of lights and darks on your sketches. Most of us do not make the darks dark enough and we have a tendency to make the lights too dark. These sketches are the "road map" used by the artist to arrive at a good painting; these road maps have very little detail, mostly tone masses. Kautzky's discussion helped me improve the value patterns in my paintings.

As time went on I noticed that many artists advertise their workshops in the art magazines (as well as by direct mail) and include a small black-and-white reproduction of their artwork. Tony Couch, for example, has been advertising his workshops this way for years. They make excellent value arrangements à la Ted Kautzky and are great studies of design; there is much to learn from these. I often refer to them during my "dry periods" to start the creative juices and ideas flowing again.

Clip the black-and-white reproductions from the magazines and mount them on mat board. I call them study boards and have expanded them to include many reproductions of artwork by other artists as well.

Black-and-white reproductions of other artists' paintings in art magazines are a good tool to teach yourself about value patterns. I clip advertisements such as these for Tony Couch workshops and save them as value studies.

JOIN A LOCAL OR REGIONAL ART GROUP

If your area or region has an art alliance of some sort, by all means join it and support it. In addition to holding lectures and educational meetings they often provide studio opportunities for members as well as membership and juried shows. I belong to several, the closest being twenty miles away, and visit it whenever I can.

One reason I joined art groups in my area is that I am interested in portrait drawing and the group's weekly morning workshops provided live models for both portrait and figure drawing. Phil Costigan taught me years ago that if you can draw portraits or figures in whatever medium, you can draw anything. Tony Couch wrote in the introduction of his book, *Watercolor: You Can Do It*, "There are no short cuts, you must practice drawing, practice, practice, practice!" And so I attended the art group's weekly morning workshop as often as I could to sharpen the powers of observation, to teach the hand and brain to work as one.

Here's another idea. Costigan also used to urge students to look at the scene, then turn their backs to it and draw it. They continue this procedure until they are satisfied with the results. Boy! This sure strengthens the powers of observation.

Kiriluk Farm Spring House,
4¾x6¾ inches,
pencil.

During a Ranulph Bye workshop we took a painting trip to Anna Kiriluk's farm in New Jersey. The chief attraction was the barn (see "Kiriluk's Barn" on page 40) and we sketched, photographed, and painted it from all angles. It was a treasure trove of textures. Before we left the area, I made the pencil sketch (at top) very quickly of the Spring House *for future use, so quickly that I forgot to photograph it. I used to have trouble converting pencil sketches into color paintings until Zoltan Szabo suggested making a series of small watercolor sketches from the pencil sketch. His suggestion solved my problem, and now I do it all the time.*

Kiriluk Farm Spring House,
7x10 inches,
watercolor sketch.

HOLD PRIVATE WORKSHOPS

Unfortunately, I eventually had to drop the figure/portrait drawing workshop because I had a conflicting commitment. But I still wanted to improve my drawing skills and to continue doing portraits. Now what?

Well, I decided to hold my own workshops by and for myself; but I soon learned that obtaining a model is difficult when you are working alone in a very small town. My solution was simple—I became my own model! All I needed was an easel, a box of pastels, two mirrors, and an assortment of hats. Why hats? Well, they provided the variety I needed; a different hat produced a different model, mood, and personality. For variety, you can alter the pose, use facial hair, use scarves; the possibilities are endless. A few of the results are shown here.

A Rembrandt I will never be, but I am able to sharpen my drawing skills as well as my imagination using this technique. I've barely scratched the surface; every now and then I get my hats and mirror out and do some practicing.

Jacob,
18×12 inches,
pastel.
Collection of Grace Biehl.

While self-portraits are fun to do, another purpose is to strengthen your powers of observation and improve your drawing skills. When you are trying to grow, and doing it alone, with no models available, use yourself. For me, the hats provide variety and, in addition, they cover my bald head. Your sketching variety is limited with a bald-headed model! You can create any number of model combinations using different hairdos, wigs, hats, scarves, jewelry, and glasses.

Butcher Stew,
18×12 inches,
pastel.
Collection of Grace Biehl.

Four Eyes Cowpoke,
18×12 inches,
pastel.
Collection of Grace Biehl.

John Wenger

John Wenger's work inspires and challenges many other artists, including me. He lives and paints in Lititz, a very small town in the heart of Pennsylvania Amish country. As I do, John loves to paint the village scene, its industries, mills, and houses, as they are and sometimes as they were before they were remodeled or demolished.

But there the similarity ends. While my style leans toward realism, his is very different. His ink line and watercolor wash sketches are architecturally correct and well drawn, but with elusive lost and found edges, lots of skips on Arches cold press paper. He lays in the washes in a loose vignette style that is both delicate and colorful, letting the colors mix on the paper.

The result is a delightful, appealing, and petite work of art...petite in that his work is painted on 9x12 or 12x16 inch watercolor blocks that you can hold on your lap while sitting at the site on a folding stool (or inside the car in cold weather). He uses a miniature paint box with six colors (cadmium red light, cadmium yellow light, yellow ochre, burnt umber, ultramarine, and alizarin crimson) to produce a spectrum of hues and values.

Do they sell? Indeed they do! There is a curious twist, though. It seems that many of his sales are to other artists (like myself), who like the watercolors because of their dainty and exquisite execution. Not too many artists have this fragile and sensitive touch. Many of us are very heavy-handed and positive with our washes and strokes. I add to my collection of Wengers every time I attend the annual art show in Lititz.

Unionville, Chester County,
by John Wenger,
7½x10 inches,
watercolor.

Horst's Mill,
by John Wenger,
9¼x13½ inches,
watercolor.

One way to challenge yourself as an artist is to study paintings by other artists whose work is different from yours. I enjoy studying Wenger's paintings because his style is not at all like mine even though his subject matter is similar.

BUILD AN IDEA FILE

Ideas can be hard to come by when you're working in isolation, so don't let any of them get away from you. I keep anything that might lead to a painting in the future in my idea file. To start your own idea file, buy several clear plastic shoe boxes and label them by subject (such as landscapes, seascapes, flowers, birds, street scenes, faces, etc.). Then accumulate tear sheets of artwork, illustrations, pictures of anything you see and admire, whether from postcards, magazines, calendars, brochures, whatever. You can easily lift the lid on the appropriate plastic box and drop in the tear sheet.

You'll use these tearsheets in dozens of ways, as references for subject matter you don't have direct access to, to compare different artists' styles and approaches to similar subjects, and for inspiration when you don't know what to paint next.

These two color sketches are among those I've placed on hold—areas that have intrigued me, subjects that I've researched and sketched that are ready to paint when the spirit moves me. Having ideas like these ready to go is a great antidote for the occasional dry spells or down periods.

DISCIPLINE

If you don't have it, you better get it. *Webster's New World Dictionary* describes it as "training that develops self-control, character, or orderliness and efficiency." If you are going to live in a small town or rural area, away from a major metropolitan center, and work alone without any artistic impetus or stimulation, then you will need discipline as Webster defined it. If you are working nine-to-five at a job not art related, discipline will help you find the time to devote to your art. You must devote some time to your art *every day*.

Every Day?

Yes...you can! Note I didn't specifically say *paint* every day (but with watercolors you can do that too)—I said some time to "your art" every day. You don't have to be at your drawing board every day, but you can mentally paint a scene while waiting in a traffic line, analyze the colors in the foggy meadow you see while driving to work, read an article or a book at break time, do some sketching at lunch time. Paint a mental portrait (and sharpen your powers of observation) whenever you are in a place with people such as the movies, church, school, play, or a concert with the kids. There is no end to the possibilities, but do *something* every day!

But I'm Not in the Mood

Everyone has dry spells or down periods. It just simply means that you must get out of the mood you are in and back into the mood to paint. So you are not in the mood to paint, okay, then don't paint. Shift gears a bit but don't abandon your art (it could take a long time until you are inspired). Get away from your watercolor board and get physical:

- Lay out and cut some mats, do some framing.

- Take a photograph safari, explore your own town again.

- Take your sketchbooks and gear for a long walk.

- Review, cull, or add to all of the idea boxes you should have by now that are filled with photographs, clippings, tear sheets, postcards, anything that will start your "imagination wheels" spinning again.

- Get out your big mirror, a box of pastels, and a group of hats, scarves, and shawls and sharpen your drawing skills by doing some self portraits.

- Start going through your library and study the works of others.

   AHA! The creative wheels are starting to turn a bit? Okay, then go back to the watercolor board again.

- Pick out one of your interesting subjects and paint it in a different way—if it's a landscape, change the mood by painting it in snow, mist, rain, fall, spring, dusk, dawn. If it's a still life, experiment with the arrangement or try different shapes. If it's a portrait, paint the person with a different expression or at a different age.

- Experiment with your materials by giving yourself new limitations. Do the painting in just two, three, or four colors, or with a one- or two-inch brush only.

- You can go on *ad infinitum*, varying your approach in any number of ways to get those creative juices flowing once again.

Older Work

As you work, study, and paint, your work will improve. As we've seen, there are many good teachers today who know how to communicate their skills to you in book form and in workshops. These presentations and your own motivation will dramatically improve your work in a short span of time. So what do you do about work that you painted and sold several years ago that is not as good as what you produce today?

I've agonized over this and finally come to a conclusion. I no longer excuse my older works because at the time I painted them, they were the best I could do. I have no guilty conscience because I was true to my art and gave it my best shot. No one can ask for more than that.

Reservoir Road,
15 x 11 inches,
pencil.

This pencil sketch is forty years old and is one of my favorites because it was influenced by Ted Kautzky, who created his sketches using a pencil sharpened not to a fine point but to a broad point. Even though you always want to improve in your painting, you never have to apologize for an earlier work if it was the best you could do at the time.

CHAPTER 4

Deciding what to paint

■ What you paint is an important decision that has to be made carefully because you want to satisfy several needs. First, the subjects have to be those that you not only enjoy painting, but can also paint well. Second, the subjects have to be those that interest your local clientele (your local market), something that they can relate to. It doesn't matter where your hometown is located—in the mountains, on the plains, or by the seashore—the principle is the same. You have to find fresh, intriguing subjects that have artistic value and will sell.

I'm not recommending that you choose subject matter and paint only those subjects you know will sell. There is nothing wrong with selling your work, but what I am recommending is that you choose what you enjoy painting, what will satisfy your artistic goals, what will help you to grow, and in addition to all that, *what you know will be salable in your market.* With a little effort on your part you can create this blend very nicely...yes, you can!

Let me tell you what I've done, why I did it, and what I've learned.

Hamburg is a small town of 4,000 people. We are an old mill town, an industrial borough with some of its factories having origins dating back to the last century. Consequently, we do not have tree-lined streets like those quaint New England villages, nor do we have the prominent courthouse squares with appropriate statuary like many lovely small Southern towns. We are not an affluent suburban borough on the outer limits of a larger metropolitan city, nor are we a bedroom community or development where the houses and public buildings were built to an architect's design. Our citizens are blue-collar people...foundry workers with leather aprons, dungarees, and dirty hands... factory workers who manufacture plowshares, batteries, brooms, and all sorts of apparel for the garment industry.

But do they buy art? *Yes, they do!* These people are mainstream America, not trained in art, but they do appreciate an image that is familiar or pleasing to them, and especially something they can relate to in a personal way; something that has touched their lives in a pleasing way. They are not interested in art that has to be explained. They know what they like.

You must do an analysis such as this of your backyard, your area, your turf. Spend some time doing a study of the people in your area. What is their income level, their social status? What cultural interests do they have—what do they like and dislike? The answers to these questions will pretty well tell you which direction to go when you paint.

Back Lot of
the Foundry,
14½x21½ inches,
watercolor.
Courtesy of Mr. and Mrs.
Edward Geschwindt.

One key to selling paintings in a small town is to paint the things that are representative of your area. You don't have to look for classic subjects such as covered bridges or seashores, either. The subject matter in a locale such as this foundry is endless.

REAL SCENES VS. IMAGINARY LANDSCAPES

Kiriluk's Barn,
15x22 inches,
watercolor.

When I began painting, I didn't know what kinds of paintings would appeal to my neighbors and potential customers. In time I got to the point where I'd produce a very good landscape or view (not just nice, but quite good) and then I'd display it with my other watercolors for sale. People would like it and would ask "Where is it?" I'd explain that it was a landscape by design, usually from the imagination. The reaction was a polite but sincere "Oh, that's nice," and the person would move on.

However, if I did a watercolor of a familiar scene or a local recognizable landmark (such as the Pennsylvania Railroad Station that has since been torn down) the reaction would be different and much more enthusiastic: "Hey, that's the old railroad station down on Second Street, the one that was torn down. How about that! Gee I'd like to have that, will you sell it? My grandfather used to work on that railroad."

After encountering this favorable reaction several times about other local views I decided to concentrate on the "village scene," the small town areas, spots, and views that could be made different, that might be dramatic, and *that I would want to do.* I know the avant-garde artists will wrinkle their noses at the idea of realistic paintings like mine, but there is room for both; the two styles can complement each other. In fact, they can support each other, both financially and artistically.

"Slopeside Farm" is a watercolor done from my imagination and designed to present an interesting picture. People liked it, but they liked "Kiriluk's Barn" better. Why? Because it was a real scene instead of an imaginary one, as you can see from the photograph. Even though the subjects are similar, the actual scene found a buyer much more quickly than the one from imagination.

Slopeside Farm,
11x15 inches,
watercolor.

Our WPA
Post Office,
14½×21½ inches,
watercolor.
Collection of Mr. and
Mrs. Terry L. Loeb.

Our post office may not be the most picturesque spot in town, but it has an interesting history. It was built during the Depression by the joint efforts of the Works Progress Administration and the Public Buildings Administration. A teller in the bank bought this painting as a gift for her husband, who is a post office clerk. Don't overlook places that are important to the people in your town just because they're not architectural wonders.

Fire Company and
Borough Hall,
21×29 inches,
watercolor.

Here's another example of the kind of scene that has proved popular with my customers. We have had fire protection in Hamburg since 1838, and this town hall and firehouse was built in 1866. The municipal offices have since been moved and a modern fire siren is used for alarms instead of the bell tower, but to its credit the fire company has preserved the bell and is proud of its many years of service.

TAKE A NEW LOOK

And so I began to re-examine my little town with a different eye. When you live in an area for a long time, you develop what I call "eyeball rut"; you see things so often that they become quite mundane. However, when you make a concentrated effort to look for something that is different, the mundane can become a thing of beauty, or at the very least a new and interesting subject for a painting. Take a walk down the alleys of your town and look for unusual angles, the play of lights and shadows. Take another look at the industries, the factories and foundries; visit their back lots (with permission, of course) that are usually full of clutter. If you like textures these areas are a veritable gold mine.

"But we don't have industries," you say. Okay, then concentrate on what you do have where you live, be it the seashore, rural farm areas, or whatever. At the shore, haunt the back bay areas, the boat yards—the potential in these areas has not been fully explored. In the rural farm areas forsake the big barns and start painting the smaller outbuildings, and then only smaller segments of these.

Once you get your "imagination wheels" spinning the ideas will flow. The igniting spark is the question, is it unusual, have I seen it before? You must remember that not every subject you choose to paint is going to become a masterpiece, but the more you try, the better your choices will become. Babe Ruth didn't hit a home run every time he came to bat; he hit a lot of singles, doubles, and triples, and they are important too, but when he did hit a home run, it was a good one!

Up until now I've suggested that you take a new look at possibilities for landscapes in the village scene or countryside. But let's take it a step further. Your study of your market or your own taste may show strong preferences for sports, flowers, nature, abstracts, and more.

Keep your eyes open to everything in your day-to-day life that might become a painting. Your neighborhood Little League games might provide the idea for a sports painting. In my area Midget Soccer and Midget Football programs are very popular. Paintings in all three areas would generate a great deal of interest locally, especially if team names show in your painting. Rather than just paint a lovely flower arrangement, why not paint the prize-winning arrangement at the local flower show? The stained glass window at church could be the basis for an abstract that people would recognize. The key element here is to paint something that people will recognize— something they can relate to.

Carversville, Solebury Township, Pennsylvania, by Ranulph Bye, 21x28 inches, watercolor.

Ranulph Bye has enjoyed enormous success by painting real scenes such as Victorian architecture and railroad depots.

Apparently people other than locals share my fascination with industries as subject matter, because this painting was not sold locally but was added to the Shippensburg University collection. Industries have so many interesting outbuildings with corners, angles, and windows, and their yards are full of clutter and textures. Look around your town for similar scenes.

Fairmount Foundry, 14½x21½ inches, watercolor. Collection of Shippensburg University.

RFD, Windsor Township, 20x24 inches, watercolor.

These five mail boxes intrigued me, so I painted them. The shapes, angles, and positions in the watercolor are how they are "in the round," but I eliminated the background and its clutter. Don't overlook smaller subjects such as these.

Cherry Blossom Time
at St. Michael's,
21½x14½ inches,
watercolor.
Collection of Mrs. Joan Wert.

Don't just look for scenes that will make wonderful paintings exactly *as they are. Remember that you can alter scenes for artistic purposes and still have the landmark recognized. This painting was commissioned by a client who gives his wife one of my watercolors for Christmas every year. They were married in St. Michael's in the spring when the cherry blossoms were in full bloom and now, years later, he wanted a watercolor to remind them of that pleasant time. There was one big obstacle—the cherry trees became diseased and were removed (see the photograph) and the client wanted me to de-emphasize the cemetery. My first sketches were horizontal, but when I changed to a vertical format, my problems were solved (see the sketch). By making similar adjustments, you can expand the number of potential subjects in your town, too.*

Plowshares
Since 1850,
14$\frac{1}{2}$x21$\frac{1}{2}$ inches,
watercolor.
Courtesy of
Mr. and Mrs. Edward Geschwindt.

The Hamburg Plow Works is a local firm that began making cast iron plowshares in 1850. Not only does it make for excellent subject matter, but the sales possibilities for paintings like this one are very good because every employee, retiree, or history buff is a potential buyer.

PLACES THAT HAVE SPECIAL MEANING

Local landmarks are instantly recognized and citizens delight in seeing these familiar places in art form. But some local buildings have more meaning to the town's residents than others. People have special attachments to places such as their churches, schools, and libraries. Some landscapes, such as a popular overlook or the local lover's lane, also have special meaning. Paintings of scenes like these will also have special meaning for the people in your town.

What are the possibilities? They're almost endless. For example, your area has many churches of various sizes and designs that can be painted in a wide variety of ways so they will not simulate a colored photograph.

Fire stations, too, are excellent subjects and there is no end to the variations that are possible. Try the station itself, or station with doors open and truck half in and half out. How about trying it with firefighters washing and polishing the equipment? Sure, it may become a Norman Rockwell-type scene, but is that all bad? Will the firefighters cooperate? Yes, they will—there is no group more faithful to their company and dedicated to service than volunteer firefighters.

I mentioned Norman Rockwell, so let's talk about him for a moment, without getting involved in the discussion of whether his work is fine art or illustration. His art is about people, lots of them, and all the stories are in his hometown—the settings are Vermont and later Massachusetts. Go to your public library and check out some of the

volumes devoted to Rockwell. There are a lot of them in circulation now, such as *Norman Rockwell's America*, Reader's Digest Edition, by Christopher Finch, published by Harry N. Abrams, Inc., New York. You might try *Norman Rockwell, Illustrator*, by Arthur Guptill, published by Watson-Guptill Publications, New York. Another good one is *The Norman Rockwell Album*, by S. Lane Faison, Jr., published by Doubleday & Co., New York. I have all three in my library, because they are excellent sources for figure studies and the settings in which they are placed. I curl up on our sofa on a rainy night with these volumes and the imagination wheels start spinning and the ideas start to flow.

Most villages have a train station that reminds residents of the "good old days." Ours has been torn down and the fact that it is no longer there creates even more nostalgia. These are excellent subjects. Ranulph Bye, AWS, NA, did a whole book devoted to *The Vanishing Depot* and it is a treasure trove of watercolors of public buildings painted in unusual and interesting formats. Paintings of scenes like these are sure to sell.

Nostalgia always strikes a responsive chord among potential buyers, and railroads especially attract attention. The Pennsylvania Railroad has dissolved and most traces of its existence are gone, so watercolors of the depot (razed in 1968) are very popular.

Pennsylvania Railroad Station, 1885-1968,
11x14 inches,
watercolor.
Courtesy of Mr. and Mrs. Richard Biehl.

Ranulph Bye

No other artist is more successful at painting scenes that hold special meanings for people than Ranulph Bye. His sensitive and skillful watercolors of the railroad industry have been incorporated into his book, *The Vanishing Depot*. His second book, *Victorian Sketchbook*, is an important record of historic and nostalgic classics of Victorian architecture. His third book, *Ranulph Bye's Bucks County*, was recently published and contains one hundred paintings of the village scenes and landmarks he knows best, and paints so well, in Bucks and Hunterdon counties.

After attending the Philadelphia Museum School of Industrial Art and the Art Students League in New York, Ranulph returned to his native Bucks County, in southeastern Pennsylvania, where his roots are deep (his family's ties to the area began with a land grant from William Penn).

There he has made a specialty of painting the village scene, historical farms and their outbuildings, famous landmarks, and vanishing architectural treasures. His paintings are not abstracts of nature—the viewer always recognizes the area or landmark, and therein lies the appeal.

If you took a photograph of the scene and compared it to the painting, you would discover that Ranulph's renditions are close (they have to be in order to be historically correct) but not exact. His eye for composition will tell him to rearrange nature a bit, and he proceeds to execute a colorful and superb watercolor of a village scene that the viewer has passed many times but has never seen in just the same way.

Ranulph Bye has earned national acclaim and has done it working in a small area. Can you do it working in your locale? Sure you can!

New Hope Station, Pennsylvania, by Ranulph Bye, 15x24 inches, watercolor.

Bucks County Playhouse, New Hope, by Ranulph Bye, 14½x21 inches, watercolor.

Bye's draftsmanship and delicate renditions of village and rural scenes capture the rich heritage of his area.

THE MUNICIPAL AREAS

Very few small towns, villages, and hamlets are built to a design. Consequently, the municipal buildings and areas were not planned but are conversions and adaptations from previously existing buildings and areas. Local residents are very proud of and loyal to their villages and hamlets and have formed attachments to these areas of nostalgia. Paintings of these sites attract a lot of interest and are salable. For example, local schools and parks are two areas that immediately come to mind...both invoke pleasant memories.

We have an unusual library—we call it our Carnegie Library because it was built in 1904 with funds donated by Andrew Carnegie, the Pittsburgh steelmaker and philanthropist. Our Borough Hall is a converted elementary school and the Senior Citizens Hall and Youth Center are housed in the former National Guard Armory. The post office built with WPA funds during the Depression is across the street and all of these buildings are located in the same block, waiting to be painted again and again. I'm sure your area has situations just as unique as these.

Education Began Here,
14x21 inches,
watercolor.

In this painting I've combined two local landmarks into one painting. The building on the left has a long local history dating back to the turn of the century, when it was used as a combined elementary and high school. It is now our local municipal offices. The building on the right is the public library, donated by philanthropist Andrew Carnegie in 1904. If you went to grade school on the left, you used the library for your assignments and had recess on the macadam play lot in between the two. Compare the painting with the photograph to see how I altered the scene to achieve a suitable composition. This scene has been very popular and I've painted it many times, varying the figures, the lighting, and the style.

VARIATIONS ON ONE SCENE

You can make the most of popular scenes like these by painting them more than once. To provide diversity, paint the scene in different seasons or moods. For example, I like to give the trees an October or November look to add color to what might be a rather plain scene. But painting that scene in winter, with snow on the ground, would create a whole different atmosphere.

Paint the same scene in daylight and at dusk, or in brilliant sunlight. Rain with its many puddles, or snow with its banks might be interesting alternatives, as well as fog or haze.

Another variation for your subject matter is to find a particular spot and paint it from many vantage points. A marine scene has these possibilities, as does an industry. Paint it from the front, the back, the side, in the yard, the street—examine it from every angle to discover the possibilities.

I've had fellow artists say to me, "How can you stand to do the same scene two or three times?" It's easy. You must remember I am suggesting that you vary it by season or mood, or even different angles, so they are not the *same identical scene.* Second, I have not suggested that you do them *back-to-back* (though I often do). Space them out as the spirit moves you.

Then, too, I have been told, "It's not really art if you do it more than once." To counter that statement, I questioned several artists who are more knowledgeable than I. At one of his workshops, Zoltan Szabo informed his students that he has done the same scene, with variations, quite often and finds no objection to it. John Pike and Phil Costigan made similar statements when questioned at their workshops. I'm not going to argue or disagree with these three great talents.

Let me share another observation. I think everyone who is remotely interested in art is aware of Andrew Wyeth's painting *Christina's World.* It is a tempera on gesso panel 32x47 inches, of Christina Olson lying in the foreground of a field looking at her farm (house and barn) in the distance on the horizon. The farm is located in Cushing, Maine, close to Andrew Wyeth's summer home. For almost three decades (1939 to 1968) Andrew Wyeth painted Christina Olson, her brother Alvaro, and their farmyard. Over the years he rendered every aspect of the house and its occupants, again and again, in quick pencil sketches, watercolors, and temperas. If thirty years of painting one subject area is acceptable to Andrew Wyeth, then it is also acceptable to me.

St. Mary's from Primrose Alley,
14¼x21½ inches,
watercolor.
Private collection.

Some subject matter lends itself to many different views and this is a good example. My first painting of St. Mary's is from Primrose Alley, and I plan another painting from this angle based on the color sketch shown here, showing the church in rain and fog. I've also painted St. Mary's as a street scene featuring the parish hall, which is used for community affairs. I always have future paintings of the same subject "on the back burner" waiting for the right time to do them.

Zoltan Szabo

When deciding what to paint, keep your eyes open for more than subject matter. You may find that what appeals to you isn't a certain type of scene but a mood or theme. Zoltan Szabo, whose paintings are in public and private collections all over the world, has said time and again, "The only real favorite of mine is not a subject but a season—winter."

Despite that preference, Szabo, who was born in Hungary and immigrated to Canada, paints a wide variety of subjects, from the most majestic landscapes to what he calls a "live still." He defines a live still as anything that can be viewed close up, such as

clumps of grass, leaves, rock formations, wild flowers, a discarded box, and so on. He paints live stills as he finds them, without meddling with or rearranging them.

Szabo, who now lives in the U.S., has written five books, produced several videos, and his workshops are always filled (I've attended two—a fascinating experience indeed). Of particular interest is *Painting Nature's Hidden Treasures,* in which he discusses his love of snow scenes and live stills and demonstrates how to paint them. (For more information, see the listings in the Resources and Bibliography sections.)

Winter Stroll,
by Zoltan Szabo,
15x22 inches,
watercolor.

Even artists as accomplished as Zoltan Szabo sometimes paint the same scene more than one time.

SCENES FROM THE PAST

Many of you may be history buffs just as I am and this opens a whole new avenue of subject matter. As I mentioned before, one of our railroad stations was torn down and I've painted it (and sold the paintings too) many times over. The second station that still exists has been altered and converted to storage space but when I paint it, I do it as it was when it was a passenger/freight station. In addition, your region may have other areas of historical value such as canals, forts, water-powered mills, and so forth. They are a challenge to do and usually sell very quickly.

You might also consider street scenes with vintage vehicles and people in period dress; still lifes of nostalgic items such as old razors, milk bottles, ice tongs, antique kitchenware, et al. The basic idea is that people have fond memories of things that are gone, and they like paintings that recapture a previous era.

Don't hesitate to take advantage of living in a small town to improve the sales potential of your paintings. Being aware of your potential customers' likes and dislikes doesn't mean selling out your artistic principles, but it can mean selling your art.

Wig Shop, 14x11 inches, ink line and watercolor wash.

Wig Shop, 11x14 inches, pencil.

Here I experimented with two styles, using the same subject. The pencil sketch is done in a style similar to Ted Kautzky; the ink line and wash painting is similar to John Wenger's style. I do this all the time to obtain a bit of variety and to grow in my painting style.

EXPLORE THE POSSIBILITIES

You may think painting subjects that have special meaning for your neighbors limits the possibilities for what you can paint. It doesn't have to. Each subject has dozens of potential paintings within it. For instance, let's single out one church and list some of the possibilities:

Interior

- Stained glass windows, realist style
- Pulpit and/or chancel area with dramatic lighting
- Abstract renditions of stained glass windows
- Still life of altar area with communion items

Exterior

- Different angles—front, sides, corners
- Four seasons—spring, summer, winter, fall
- Steeple or bell tower
- Doors

Martin Kaercher's
Stone at St. John's,
14¼x21¼ inches,
watercolor.
Collection of
Mr. and Mrs. M. Domer Leibensperger.

Every subject offers dozens of possibilities—but you may have to look for them. I'd walked (and driven) south on Church Street almost daily for years and never thought of this view of St. John's as a painting subject. Late one afternoon as I passed, the long shadows were cast on the mountain stone, a memorial to the founder of Hamburg in 1772, and gave me the idea for this painting. I painted the church steeple another time, and have painted other watercolors based on this scene. Even if you paint abstracts or still lifes, a setting like this one can provide inspiration if you explore it.

St. John's Steeple,
14x11 inches,
watercolor.

Paint any and all of these in a wide variety of modes and in whatever style meets your artistic goal.

I've listed several possibilities for just one church; now multiply those by the number of churches in your vicinity. What is the market potential for these? Consider the number of churches times the membership of each one.

I'm not urging you to paint the above list of possibilities in a methodical fashion. I'm merely suggesting that this is what can be done, that there is a market for these paintings. Parishioners love their churches. I've had clients who purchased a painting of their church for themselves and clients who purchased a painting of their church and donated it to the church to be displayed along with other mementos. Some clients did not want to purchase a 22x30 or 15x22 watercolor of the church but opted instead for a smaller 11x15 painting of the steeple or the door.

Paint from this list of possibilities only *if you want to paint them.* The subject matter must appeal to you, must be an artistic challenge, must meet your artistic objectives, and must reflect your personal expression. If your painting does all of the above, and then sells too (and it will), you will be a two-fold winner.

If you don't want to paint churches, use this same principle to paint something that *does* appeal to you—choose a subject that has special meaning for people in your community and explore all the possibilities for painting that subject.

This watercolor is unusual for a number of reasons. You don't often see "five- and ten-cent stores" anymore, but this one is truly an ageless gem, started at the turn of the century by the present owner's grandparents. Visitors to our town love to shop this old-timer, and natives fondly recall how they used to get the biggest and creamiest ice cream cones for a dime. The red-and-white tile facade is gone now (see the photo), but I painted this from an old photograph to recapture the old days for the Miller family.

Miller's 5-10-1.00 Store,
14½x21½ inches,
watercolor.
Collection of
Dr. and Mrs. George Miller.

CHAPTER 5

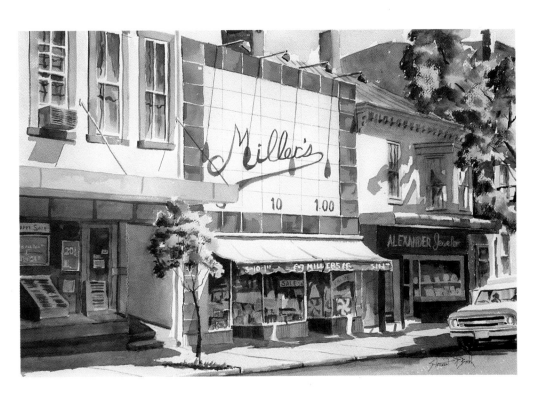

How to please the small town buyer

■ Is the small town art buyer different than the large city buyer? Yes, I think there is a big difference. A general and simplified statement describing this difference would be that the urban art buyer more readily accepts intellectual or artistic experimentation in addition to the conservative and traditional forms of art. Small town art buyers (even though a lot of them migrated from the city) lean more toward realism, with a little abstraction on the side. This buyer usually has little enthusiasm for avant-garde forms of expression.

I don't feel fully qualified to analyze the tastes of the large city art buyer because I haven't made a thorough analysis of the city market, even though we did live in metropolitan Philadelphia for several years.

However, I am quite comfortable in a discussion about small town buyers. The majority of my life has been spent in this type of environment. In addition, I have made an in-depth analysis of the people in my local market, such as I urged you to do in Chapter 4.

Simply stated, the small town and rural art buyers are not interested in art that has to be explained or interpreted. Usually they are not art trained, but these buyers know what they like and do appreciate forms and shapes expressed in artistic fashion that are both colorful and pleasing to the eye. They are not concerned about 'isms and avant-garde theories of paintings; they prefer traditional approaches, possibly leaning toward a touch of photo-realism.

The Tulip Tree is in Bloom,
14¼ x 21¼ inches,
watercolor.
Collection of Dr. and Mrs. Clifford Wagner.

This watercolor has many elements that not only please the eye of the beholder, but also were incorporated to please the owner. The home itself has quite a history and now contains both the residence and professional offices of the owner. The lovely tulip tree in the backyard is much admired when in bloom, so I made a point of painting the tree at the height of its beauty. A portion of the home across the street also was included because it is the home of an ancestor.

COMMISSIONS

Small town art buyers like paintings of subject matter they can relate to—subject matter that has touched their lives. This explains why I get a lot of requests for commissions. Many artists don't care to do commissions—they feel it dulls their creative edge, stifles their artistic flow. I can respect that. However, commissions need not become schlock art if you handle them properly and don't lose sight of the fact that they can be lucrative...and I enjoy making deposits in the bank.

I accept commissions, but not blindly. My guess is that 80 percent of the paintings I do are about subject matter of my choosing; these are paintings that I wanted to do for many and various reasons such as mood, patterns, history, textures, lights and shadows, etc. The other 20 percent is by commission and most of those are "house portraits," paintings of the client's home or place of business. I usually tell a client who wants to commission a painting that I must look at and study what it is they want me to paint. If it is a subject that is better served by a photograph, or that doesn't appeal to me, then I'm not interested and turn it down.

What to Discuss with the Client

Commissions can be a pleasant experience and not a source of irritation if you handle some things up front. It is important that you discuss a number of areas before you start and in so doing anticipate problem areas and sidestep them. You also gain valuable information that will help you produce a good end result. Sure, we always want to turn out a "blue ribbon painting" no matter what our subject matter or circum-

stances, but in the case of commissions it is particularly important. Why? I've found that *nine out of ten of my commissions lead to a second commission or sale and sometimes more.* Yes, 90 percent!

During the discussion about the commission I usually am able to learn if there is some special feature about the home that the client is particularly proud of. For example, one husband told me that his wife's pride and joy was the pink tulip tree on the north side of their home. Another had a prized blooming pear tree. Still another pointed out the newly repolished hardware on the front door. Listen for similar clues from your clients. Someone who wants a portrait

of their child may comment on the child's beautiful eyes, or a client who plans to hang your work in a certain room may want you to use certain colors (be careful of requests such as these). Don't surrender your artistic control, but if you can accommodate the client, why not do so?

I seldom submit preliminary sketches or diagrams to the client for review even though some request that I do. That can get to be quite a hassle. When I agree to do the painting I explain to the client that I have looked at their home and I will paint it, but I do want them to understand that I will paint it my way, with my choice of view or angle, season, or mood.

Joan's Back Porch,
14½ x 21½ inches,
watercolor.
Collection of Mrs. Joan Wert.

The client who commissioned this painting of his wife's childhood home just told me, "Do what you can." The house is a very lovely old stone home, but the contour of the land and proximity of the farm's outbuildings ruled out a front view. However, all traffic in a farm house ebbs and flows through the back door and the rear view of the house was more accessible. So I made a few sketches, cleared away some of the hanging pine boughs and this was the result.

I also explain that I would like permission to show the painting if the occasion presents itself, and I have shown commissioned paintings at juried shows as well as neighborhood shows. My request has never been turned down. Clients are proud of their paintings—don't forget, the subject matter is their pride and joy; otherwise they would not have had a watercolor commissioned in the first place. They love to have it displayed with other paintings, so they can share their pride with friends and neighbors.

This desire to share their pride with others is important to you, too. As I pointed out before, nine out of ten commissions lead to another sale

of some kind. Most of these sales come when a client shows off a painting I've done to a friend or relative.

When I sell a painting of the village scene, and especially a building or scene that is of interest to more than one person (such as a historical building like the torn-down railroad station), I always explain that I reserve the right to paint that area, scene, or subject again, *but always different*...different angle, mood, season, or lighting. That way, if a client later sees another painting of the same scene, he or she won't be surprised or feel I misrepresented myself. No one has ever objected to this.

Bausher-Baney House,
Circa 1914,
14³/₄x21³/₄ inches,
watercolor.
Collection of Dr. and
Mrs. Charles Baney.

The owners of this painting enjoyed it so much they commissioned a painting of the house for each of their three grown children, who live in other parts of the country, to remind them of their roots. You may think it would be boring to paint four portraits of the same house, but you can add variety by making big changes, such as the point of view, or minor changes, such as the figures, auto, tree on the left side, and subtle elements like the curtain treatment.

Heinly-Flickinger House,
Circa 1865,
14$\frac{1}{4}$ x 21$\frac{1}{4}$ inches,
watercolor.
Collection of
Mr. and Mrs. John Flickinger.

*Sometimes a client's wishes are
impractical as well as downright
impossible to achieve. In cases
such as these your expertise must
prevail. For example, this client
asked me to include details such as
the newly refinished hardware on
the front door, gingerbread, and
scrollwork in a portrait of his
home. I told him it wasn't possible
to include all those details, and
suggested a montage of those
special points as a second painting. He said yes, and he and his
wife loved both paintings.*

Heinly-Flickinger House Montage,
14$\frac{1}{4}$ x 21$\frac{1}{4}$ inches,
watercolor.
Collection of Mr. and Mrs. John Flickinger.

One of the local professional men, a repeat client and supporter of the arts, approached me one day and asked if I'd take a look at his mountain home (about an hour's drive away) and render my impression in watercolor. I agreed to look, but told him I reserved the right to portray it "my way." When I saw the chalet (see photo) it cried out to me SNOW! So that's how I painted it, and the painting was well received. When the next snow came I drove up to the chalet to see how nature painted the scene and was satisfied with my way.

Charlie's Shangri La,
21 x 27 inches,
watercolor.
Collection of Dr. and Mrs.
Charles Baney.

When deciding whether to accept a commission, don't turn down a job just because it's unusual or difficult. The president of the Hamburg Broom Works approached me with one of the company's 1914 advertising booklets that had an image of the plant on the back cover and asked me to produce a watercolor from it. The image was a line engraving the size of a business card (see photo) and they had no photographs of the plant at that time. My first impulse was to turn it down, but the challenge overpowered my hesitation. After studying the line engraving with a magnifying glass and playing around with several sketches I realized the project was possible. The president was so delighted he bought the watercolor for his personal collection and the project led to the purchase of several more of my watercolors for the corporate collection as well as that of the president.

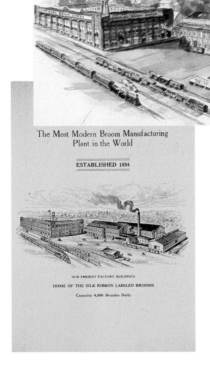

Hamburg Broom Works,
Circa 1912,
14½ x 21½ inches,
watercolor.
Collection of Thomas Baver.

SPECIALTIES

They may not admit it, but most artists like to paint one style of painting or subject matter more than others: flowers, still lifes, clouds, barns, portraits, or whatever. I call them specialties. If you have such inclinations then by all means develop them. A specialty can help you build a reputation, then you can branch out from there. Also, developing a specialty that takes into account the particular interests of the people in your region makes sales easier.

Is developing a specialty limiting yourself? Not at all. Does it stifle your creative development? Certainly not. It can help provide financial support so you can continue your artistic development in other areas. I'm not saying you have to paint your specialties 100 percent of the time.

My specialty happens to be the village scene, but this doesn't mean that I am urging you to do *exactly the same thing.* You may have another specialty. For instance, I have a friend who paints birds and does it very well. She produces lovely 11x14-inch watercolor studies of all types of birds from the large majestic birds of prey to the tiny energetic wrens and finches. Her renditions are delicate, believable, and delightful—bird watchers love them.

Every area has a group of bird watchers; for example, our area has a rather large group of nature and bird watchers because of our proximity to Hawk Mountain Sanctuary, a nationally known sanctuary developed to provide a haven for all forms of wildlife with special emphasis on the birds of prey. Birders are a special breed of nature

Blue Bird,
by Mary C. Schappell,
11x14 inches,
watercolor.

Mary Schappell is a birder and has been since her youth. After she retired she decided she wanted to do more than just look at and study birds, so she started taking lessons from wildlife artist Frederick William Wetzel and her talent blossomed. Here is a great-grand-mother who is developing a specialty and doing it very well. Can you do it too? Yes, you can.

lovers and are very supportive of the arts.

Another specialty that can be developed in a small town is pet portraiture. The owners of these animals are of a special stripe…the love and devotion that they shower on their animals is beyond belief. You have only to visit an area horse show or dog show and observe the care and affection that is extended to the animals to realize there is a market for an artist's paintings of these fine animals. A color photograph is fine, but an artistic rendition is even better.

Children's portraiture is another lucrative specialty you might consider. If you have a flair and an interest in portraiture, by all means develop this interest. This too is a cash-producing field.

All these specialties are great fun to do and they do produce a cash flow. As I said, you don't have to devote all your painting energies to a specialty; however, a specialty painting does attract a clientele that will buy this type of painting quicker than

they would a beautiful landscape or an interesting abstract. Look at it this way: Many times the sale of a special painting does support the habit, buys the supplies, and provides the money that will permit you to work on other subject matter that might provide more artistic satisfaction but just doesn't sell as rapidly.

Eric Sloane painted so many barns that he became known as "the Barn Man." He also had another specialty, clouds and skies. These specialties supported all his other artistic projects. Ted Kautzky was a celebrated watercolorist but in addition he had a specialty that was pencil renditions of planned construction sites. John Pike used to refer to himself as the "fog and water boy." I'm not going to quarrel with any of these three great talents.

PAINTING THE HOUSE PORTRAIT

As I said, my specialty is painting the village scene, including what I call the house portrait. This is a painting of someone's dwelling; the house may be large and ornate or small and comfortable. In any event, to them it is home, a place of which they are very proud, so much so that they want a watercolor rendition of it. It may even be a vacation cottage or a place of business but in any event it has a special meaning to the client. To paint house portraits, you must take the mundane and keep it recognizable, yet different from a photograph, by adding interesting shadows, colors, angles, seasons, whatever.

People love house portraits—for many reasons. Husbands have commissioned paintings such as this for their wives' birthdays, anniversaries, Valentine's Day, and Christmas, as well as other holidays. Wives have purchased them for husbands for similar reasons. Friends often commission a painting to be used as a wedding present or retirement gift. Children have presented the paintings to their parents at anniversary time. Parents have commissioned paintings of their homes for their children who now live in another section of the country. It reminds them of their roots and helps them remember that this is a large storehouse of memories…memories they don't want to forget.

Twenty-two North Fourth Street,
15x22 inches,
watercolor.
Collection of
Dr. and Mrs. David Geiger.

This townhouse is almost in the center of town and made for a very interesting study of door and windows, which provided the variety needed for a rather plain facade. It wasn't a commission—I painted it because it was of interest to me. The fact that it sold made the effort even more rewarding.

The Challenge of Outdoor Subjects

When painting the village scene or any other subject outdoors in a small town, you encounter some unique problems that don't confront you out in the countryside. When you're in town, you are very visible and are in the center of traffic and activity. Obviously you cannot deposit your gear and set up your easel on the sidewalk of the downtown business section and start to sketch or paint the scene before you. You interfere with traffic, both vehicular and pedestrian, and you invite all kinds of interruption and comment from passersby. I cannot work that way because of these distractions. It looks very arty and does help to create a favorable image but that is not for me.

Some people can paint that way…if you can, by all means do it. Several summers ago we visited a tourist town in the West and one of the local artists was painting simple quarter-sheet sketches with ink line and splashy washes of the street scene before him. He attracted a crowd and seemed to enjoy it. He also sold every wash sketch as soon as he completed it. I bought several…I liked them!

So What Can You Do?

To get around the problem of working in public, I take as many photographs (both slide and print form) as I can and do most of my work in my studio. But taking photos isn't always easy, either. Parked cars and the flow of traffic often interfere. I find that the best time to go afield with my camera in the town itself is on a Sunday morning. Traffic is always at a minimum and the

Alma's House,
11x15 inches,
watercolor.
Courtesy of Alma Shollenberger.

These two houses are alongside each other on North Fifth, and they both posed a similar challenge: I couldn't take reference photos from which to work because the street is tree-lined. I had to wait until enough leaves fell that I could see the details of the houses. Both paintings were commissioned, but for different reasons. The Kamps had just bought the house and were moving into the neighborhood to begin a new life. "Alma's House" was commissioned by a devoted friend because Alma had sold the house in which she grew up and was leaving the neighborhood to move into a retirement home.

few parked cars you do encounter usually don't interfere.

However, restricting your camera activity to one day a week poses a new set of problems—light and weather. Sometimes you have to wait quite a few Sundays before you have the light you want; I favor early morning because of those long shadows. Sometimes the subject has a tree or two that shades the building and blocks the view. I've had to wait several months until leaves fall so I can get the proper view. You either have to be patient or be able to imagine the scene with the lighting you want.

The Camera Alone Is Not Enough
In addition to using the camera, I like to make a few simple sketches, sometimes black and white and sometimes in color. These are made from my car or some other inconspicuous vantage point. The sketches are usually made of several parts of the subject, such as doorways, windows, or dormer construction and they serve a twofold purpose. First, they provide detail that is often missed by the camera.

But second, and more im-portant, doing the sketch increases my awareness of the subject. Taking a few quick camera snaps does not expose you to your subject long enough. Taking the time to do a few simple sketches will increase your powers to recall the scene. Remember those self-portrait drawing drills? Re-member those sketching drills when you observed and then turned your back to draw? That training was for this type of sketching and drawing.

The Kamps Bought It,
15x22 inches,
watercolor.
Courtesy of
Mr. and Mrs. Richard F. Kamp.

Making Sketches

Making photographs or sketches of a person's home presents a different set of problems. Paintings like this often are commissioned by someone who wants to present it to a spouse, parents, or special friends as a *surprise gift* on a special day, be it anniversary, holiday, or whatever. Since it is a surprise you cannot be visible when taking your photographs and doing your sketching; someone may be home. I always discuss this with a client and obtain a schedule of comings and goings of the occupants of the home.

Neighbors also have to be considered. In these days of spreading vandalism and break-ins, neighbors by mutual consent keep an eye on each other's property. I've had neighbors come to me while I was taking pictures and want to know if I was a real estate agent…are they selling? I've been asked if I was from the tax assessor's office…is the neighborhood being re-assessed? I've had neighbors tell my client's family that "Stew Biehl was taking pictures of your house and then sat in his car for half an hour writing in a notebook…is something going on?" Then the surprise is gone!

I discuss this with the client too. I usually recommend that they make the neighbors aware that I will be in the neighborhood *and why*. This works well for two reasons. First, the neighbors enjoy being a part of the plot (they want to see it when it is finished) and they love to let the recipient know that they knew about the surprise. Second, they get to see the painting and have a personal interest in it—so much so that this secrecy and minor involvement often has led to another commission. One thing leads to another, but more about that later.

Local Flavor

Be sure to put plenty of local flavor into your paintings. Since ours is an industrial town I usually include the narrow pavements, the parking and street signs, the utility poles with transformers, as well as the overhead transmission lines and service lines. Included too are the overhead traffic signal lights as well as the painted walkway lanes at the street corners. All these elements tell the viewer where they are and what kind of place it is.

I don't faithfully include *everything*…just enough of the power lines, utility poles, fire hydrants, and so forth to fit into the picture artistically to convey the flavor of Hamburg. Someone once asked me whether we ever get comments from people who say, "Why did you put that ugly power line in there; do you ever lose sales because of that?" No, I never

Here's a perfect example of why a photograph alone is not enough of a reference. The tree and fountain in the right corner were out of the camera's field of view, but when I sketched the scene I moved them closer to the corner and later included them in the painting. As you walk north on Third Street your eye sees the tree, fountain, and church as one scene, but the camera did not. This composition also provides more balance than the scene recorded by the camera.

Bethany United Methodist Church,
22x30 inches,
watercolor.

had anyone ask me why and no, I never lost a sale because of that. And now that the subject of lost sales has been introduced, I'd like to add that I never had a client who did not like, or refused, a completed commission.

If your locality is the shoreline, the tree-shaded New England village, the rural town in the Midwest, or the desert small town of the West, then by all means be sure to include all those individual elements that subconsciously tell the viewer where they are.

Some time ago I decided that almost all my paintings should have some form of life in them; could be a flock of birds, an animal or two, but usually some people. The figures are incidental to the picture's composition, but their inclusion does add human interest and an element of life that does exist in the village scene. The books *Putting People in Your Paintings* and *People Painting Scrapbook,* by Everett Draper, will help you to accomplish this. (If you're not comfortable drawing people, see Chapter 2 for an easy way to transfer drawings of figures onto your main drawing.)

Daniel Dinkel Home, 15x22 inches, watercolor.

I try to include some form of life in all my house portraits, such as the mailman walking along the brick pavement here, to give a sense of the lives going on inside. This home is across the street from the Shrom house, which I painted with a young couple outside because many young people visited the Shroms' two daughters when they were home.

The Shrom Family Home, 15x22 inches, watercolor.

This painting includes small nuances of local flavor. This house is close to the street, as was customary in towns like ours one hundred years or so ago, so I included the sidewalk with people, the utility pole and wires to convey that feeling. (Permit me to include a personal note: The red house behind the utility pole is ours.)

CHAPTER 6

How to promote and sell your paintings

■ Many artists are fortunate enough to have had their formal training in a major metropolitan center at one of the many universities, colleges, or art schools located there. After they have completed their formal training they work in an art-related field to sustain themselves while they continue to paint whenever they can. Because of their location they are close to and work with other artists who are at the same level of development. In addition, they are exposed to professionals who are at an even greater stage of accomplishment. This has a very positive effect on their own development and allows them to make the contacts required to sell their work in that metropolitan (yes, even national) market.

This is fine! But if you live outside these metropolitan areas—if you're part of rural America made up of the villages and hamlets of small town life—you'll have to find different ways to market your work.

For the purposes of this chapter I am going to assume that you live in the country or a small town, and that you are still growing artistically but have not as yet made agent or gallery connections that will ultimately market your paintings nationally, or at least on a broad regional level. In fact, your "rural America" usually doesn't even have a gallery that will sell your work. So what do you do? How do you promote your work?

PROMOTE YOURSELF AS WELL AS YOUR ART

If you are going to paint and sell your paintings in a small town (or rural area) then you've got to spread your image, your reputation as an artist. Your goal is to let the public in your area know who you are and what you do. When the public thinks of art, you want them to think of you. When the public wants to buy art, you want them to think of you.

To do that, you must promote your hometown. You must become active and participate in its affairs: *You must be a part of it!* How do you do this? It's easy!

You don't necessarily have to do everything that is suggested in the following text but at least do a part of it. This is what has worked for me; but you are a creative person too and can be innovative enough to find even more or different ways to accomplish your goal.

This bank, founded in 1872, has been through five expansions and commissioned me to paint a series showing each stage of growth. While doing this commission, I developed a good working relationship with the bank officers, who are committed to helping local artists and craftspeople. Their last expansion included the former jewelry store in the lower right corner, and they have preserved the window to provide display space for artists' work. It is here that I exhibit 90 percent of my work.

Hamburg Savings & Trust Co., 22x30 inches, watercolor.

BECOME PART OF THE COMMUNITY

A good way to become part of your town is through civic, social, and religious organizations. All these groups offer ways to meet others in your town and get to know them while doing something for the town. Be conscious of the service-oriented clubs and groups in your area. There are many: Rotary, Exchange, Kiwanis, Lions, Sertoma, Business and Professional Women, Women's Clubs, Jaycees, and so many others. (By the way, many of these clubs were once male oriented. Now they almost all open their doors to women. If not yet, they will—you could be the one to break that barrier.)

You should also be informed of the fire companies, ambulance corps, environmental and ecology groups, agricultural clubs (such as the Grange), and a whole host of similar social organizations in your area.

Also, be mindful of the churches and their Sunday schools. These institutions, too, have a large number of supporting organizations.

All these organizations are always looking for programs, and here is a good opportunity for you to make these organizations *aware of you.*

Give Demonstrations and Speeches

Do a demonstration for your club or organization! It's a great way to increase your visibility in the community.

There are several things you can do as a demonstration, such as a quickie pastel portrait of a member. If you need more than half an hour, complete a pastel portrait before the meeting and then during the program portion, explain what you did and why, step by step. Show a completed watercolor and do a critique; take the members through the painting procedure step by step, from sketch to mat and frame, discussing design, values, colors, etc. All of these are entertaining and educational for club members, and help build your reputation as an artist.

If you are uncomfortable with doing a demonstration, develop a talk or presentation on art history, appreciation, or any other subject in this area that you are familiar with. You could develop a program devoted to ways that art can enrich people's lives.

Show the audience, without being too obvious, how objects of art (your art) can enhance their office spaces, their homes, and the homes of their friends and relatives. Show them how and why objects of art (your art) are greatly appreciated and very appropriate as presentations for special occasions, those times when an ordinary gift will not do. That list is long—weddings, anniversaries, retirements, *ad infinitum.*

Clubs don't often get speakers who cover topics such as this and the average person will quickly protest that he has no interest in this area, "Why, I can't even draw a straight line with a ruler," they will exclaim. But they are interested, they are curious. Their self-professed lack of interest is a facade they have set up to shield their lack of knowledge. You can awaken this latent interest in art—it lies dormant within everyone.

There is no end to the topic possibilities and combinations available. With some thought and energy you can create and develop a whole range of presentations that will let your audiences know who you are and what you do. With these variations you can do this again, and again, and yet again, without being pushy.

Keep your presentations light and breezy, but end on a serious note and let them know that art is preserved for society, not by the common stereotyped image of the long-haired starving artist or the stuffy museum, but by the interest and support of people such as themselves.

Eventually when all of these people think of art, they will think of you. As they are exposed to art at galleries or mall shows, they will recall what you explained or shared with them. *They will think of you...* and favorably so...and this translates into sales. When customers buy a piece of art they do so because they appreciate it as a piece of art. However, they also like it even more when they enjoy a rapport with the artist. As buyers proudly show their purchases to friends they also like to share their favorable information about the artist.

Write a Column

Another way to keep your name before the public in a favorable way is to develop and write a short column for the local weekly newspaper. The dailies usually have a staff person assigned to this topic, but the newsy little local weeklies are not that affluent and most of the times are receptive to a freelance column devoted to all aspects of art—painting, framing, decorating, appreciation, shows and exhibits, etc.

Lynda K. Potter

Lynda Potter, an accomplished watercolorist living in Bluffton, South Carolina, is ever mindful of the churches and other organizations looking for unusual and different presentations. After lengthy research, she prepared and presents an illustrated lecture titled, "Images of Christ in the Fine Arts," which explains different artistic interpretations of Christ's image, including those from different countries, cultures, and sects.

The title alone sets one's imagination into motion and you can understand that she would be hard-pressed to squeeze her material into one hour. Another program equally as fascinating is "Symbolism of Christianity in Fine Arts," and she is currently researching and developing a third program tentatively titled, "Women in Fine Arts."

Linda's artistic achievements include a long list of invitational, juried, as well as solo exhibitions in several media—oil, pastel, and watercolor. Her background also includes stints of teaching adult watercolor classes, for which she is well qualified.

In addition, Linda is an active volunteer. Her artistic and organizational skills are utilized by a diverse list of organizations in her area, from serving as a volunteer teacher's aide at the elementary school level to serving as a board member of the President's Arts and Cultural Council at Alvernia College and judging various local art shows, to serving as chairperson for government studies for the League of Women Voters.

Why get so deeply involved? Because when she exposes her abilities and talents to this wide sphere of people she not only gives but also receives, and the experiences are most rewarding. There is one additional fringe benefit— eventually when these people with whom she is in contact think of art, they will think of her.

Self Portrait,
by Lynda Potter,
22x30 inches,
graphite.

Festiva Maxima,
by Lynda Potter,
15x22 inches,
watercolor.

Frederick William Wetzel

Teaching has been a major part of Fred Wetzel's life. A naturalist, ornithologist, and artist, Fred shares his knowledge of biology with students at all grade levels and his artistic talents through his School of Wildlife Arts and Related Studies.

Fred came to teach art in a roundabout way. In his youth, he lived in the countryside of Allentown, Pennsylvania, and in his junior high school years a teacher opened his eyes to the sights and sounds of the out-of-doors. He was exposed to the mysteries and beauty of birds in flight. He began to paint, seeing in feathers the subtle textures of watercolors.

After receiving his bachelor of science in biology, Fred continued his study of ornithology, specializing in birds of prey. This led to a position with Hawk Mountain Sanctuary in Kempton, Pennsylvania, where he served as assistant curator. While there, he did pen-and-ink illustrations for the book *View from Hawk Mountain*, published by Scribner's.

Even though Fred received some art instruction from Conrad Roland (who was a student of Louis Agassiz Fuertes), he is largely self taught. Perhaps that's why his approach to teaching art is different than most. His classes, taught from his studio near Kempton, are not the usual three- or four-day workshops for twenty to thirty students. He conducts a weeklong session of concentrated personal attention. Initially he had six students in his classes but found that size a bit unwieldy so he now limits class sizes to four. (For more information, see page 133.)

Rough-Legged Hawk, by Frederick William Wetzel, 15x20 inches, watercolor.

Since it was a teacher who introduced Fred to the wonders of nature that led to his successes as an ornithologist and wildlife painter, it seems appropriate that he now shares this talent and specialty with students interested in the same field.

As Fred did, you may find that teaching serves as a perfect complement to painting. It can be challenging and rewarding!

WHY NOT TEACH A CLASS?

There may not be an art class in your area—if there isn't, then you start one. You may not feel that you are advanced enough to teach a class, but remember that there are other would-be artists out there who may not have as much experience as you do and would be glad to learn the basics. They might even prefer to start out with someone who's not so advanced that they feel intimidated.

Teaching a class can help establish your artistic reputation around town, as well as generate a bit of income. You may also find that it helps you learn and grow through contact with other artists.

If you are not comfortable with *teaching* a class, then start a group workshop. Organize a group that can meet for a couple of hours on a regular schedule in whatever space you can find—maybe a room in the youth center, the library, or even in a basement room of the church.

I had a friend who used to do this. She organized a workshop group and served as facilitator and leader. She didn't feel capable of being the instructor, but was able to keep the group working in one steady direction. She arranged for space in a church basement, accumulated material for still-life subjects, and motivated interest and attendance. A simple monetary collection was made and she donated this to the church.

With a little energy she accomplished several objectives. She got more embryo artists out of their silent corners, working together, and (most important) exchanging ideas. She grew too, artistically and image-wise, and she also made a financial contribution to the church whose facilities they used. On occasion they were able to import a professional artist who helped solve some of their problems and conducted critiques.

Did it take time? Sure it did, but she was compensated by an enhanced image—she became known as Ms. Art, which led to several sales that would not have been made otherwise. It is good public relations!

DISPLAY YOUR ART

In addition to making yourself visible, you must also make your art visible. *You must display your work.* If you don't have gallery representation (there may not even be any galleries available in your regional market), your buyers can't come from gallery traffic, which is usually made up of people seeking art. Your potential buyer is the person in the street. So your work must be displayed where there is traffic, where the largest number of people will see it.

Now here you have to do some research. You must review whatever spaces *might be available,* just possibilities, and then study traffic patterns both pedestrian and vehicular to find out where you'll get the most exposure. Run the following suggestions through your mental computer.

The Bank Lobby
Banks are very community minded and also supportive of the arts. Their lobbies make wonderful places to display your art as they're always full of people.

Sometimes lobby walls are available for your display but I lean toward using a free-standing A-frame peg-board display that you either buy or make yourself. Keep it small and simple—by small I mean thirty-six inches wide and sixty inches high so you don't monopolize too much space in the lobby, and simple so one person can carry it in and out. The bank custodian will be grateful too if it is simple to move during cleaning.

Your work will be at pedestrian level, low enough for children to touch and finger, so do not use frames or glass. It is too easy to damage or break the glass. Instead, I use shrink-wrap (or you can use plastic wrap) so your work won't be finger-soiled by the youngsters. Remember, the bank hands out lollipops, too.

Put two simple signs on the board. One tells the viewer who you are and how you can be reached by address and telephone. I don't recommend putting prices on the sign because I don't expect the bank to handle sales and field questions.

On the second sign tell the viewer something like this, "This space has been graciously made available by (name of the bank)...a local bank, with local employees, and a long history of service to local people." This second sign tells the public that the bank was kind enough to let you use its space; it is your way of saying thank you and is good public relations. You might remember to include a small sign such as this wherever you display your paintings, be it banks, retail windows, restaurants, wherever.

Retail Store Windows
Obviously these spaces attract attention because merchants place their merchandise in them too. This is premium space and sometimes they

don't like to share any of it. However, sometimes they will make space available because of the local flavor of your artwork and the interest it engenders. If your research indicates that a particular store window would be ideal, don't be afraid to ask—you might be surprised at the response, and if you don't ask you'll never know.

Restaurants

I've never used a restaurant but if there wasn't a better space available, I'd at least try it. A lot of restaurants have trial paintings on their walls, but you must gauge the worth of exhibiting in a particular restaurant by actually exhibiting your work and evaluating the results.

The Local Medical Center

We have a facility known as the Hamburg Family Practice Center, which is run by several doctors. Its lobby, halls, and offices are great showcases for local artwork. You will find the medical and dental professions are very supportive of the arts. They not only make their walls available for display purposes on a rotating basis but they also buy works of art for their personal collections.

Try approaching the medical professionals in your town and ask if they'll allow you to display your work in their offices. Many times they are glad to have something on the walls to brighten up waiting rooms and corridors.

Where Else?

How about the village library, or the windows of your local insurance agency, the dry cleaners—*wherever there is traffic!* This is why your analysis of your village pedestrian traffic is so important.

Let me repeat, you must display your paintings where as many people as possible will look at them. What kind of people? All sorts of people. Some will be interested just because they like "pretty pictures." Some will admire the scene and try to figure out where it is. Others will try to remember who you are. Still others tuck what they see away in their memory banks and maybe contact you some months later with a request for a commission; and then, too, some are really interested and *buy!*

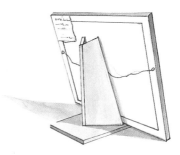

I use a simple homemade stand like this one to display my art in store windows. It's 13 inches tall, with a base that's 8x10 inches. A small ledge along the front edge keeps the painting upright.

Hamburg Family Practice Center,
15x22 inches,
watercolor.

The professional community of any area is usually very supportive of the arts. The Hamburg Family Practice Center, which purchased this painting for its reception room, allows local artists to display their work in waiting rooms, offices, and corridors. It is a busy place with a constant flow of patients and these displays attract plenty of attention and comment.

Regina Dancull Gouger

Sometimes a casual interest or hobby can combine with a love of art to produce an unusual twist. A perfect example is the work of Regina Gouger— Ginger to her friends.

A watercolorist who loves to paint florals and nature studies, Ginger also enjoys needlework. With some creative thinking, she found a way to combine the two, using her original watercolors to create patterns for cross-stitch and needlepoint.

The process works like this: First, the watercolor is traced. Then, using a light table and graph paper, the tracing is transformed into a graphed drawing. Colored threads are selected to match the colors used in the painting and each thread is given a symbol that will identify it on the graph. When the stitcher follows the graph and symbols, the result is a re-creation of the original watercolor.

This sideline grew to the point where Ginger established her own company, Ginger & Spice, which now has sales throughout the United States, as well as in New Zea-land, Canada, and Australia.

Can you convert your major interest or specialty into fun and profit? Sure you can! Don't mimic Ginger—let your creative juices flow and come up with your own unique approach.

Broken Lanterns,
by Regina Dancull Gouger,
watercolor.

Autumn Lanterns,
by Regina Dancull Gouger,
needlework.

Will People Look?

The bank at which I display my paintings bought a neighboring jewelry store and converted the inside space to office use. They retained one of the jewelry display windows to be used to display local art and to show locally made crafts, as well as local products made and sold by some of their business customers. And do people see the art in that window? You better believe it...the response has been terrific! Now let me define that. I don't mean that everything put in there has been sold. A lot of it has and I am very grateful for that, but in addition, I've had a lot of favorable comments, questions, discussions, and inquiries about work for the future. One can't ask for more than that.

Hints for Displaying Art

I've learned a few things about displaying artwork that I'd like to pass along. Don't overcrowd the space. Initially I tried to get too many paintings in the window. Now I find that it is more effective if I limit my pieces to no more than four. Rotate them frequently—don't keep them in the space more than two weeks. As you rotate them you can return the first ones again later in the cycle.

In setting up the display, I use a simple tabletop easel that I made myself. I usually do not frame the paintings, but mount the watercolors on a piece of foam-core, cover them with a simple mat, and then cover the whole with shrink-wrap. (More about that in Chapter 7.)

PAINT A SERIES

Once you have found a location or place to display your work on an ongoing basis, you can help draw people to that spot by featuring your paintings as a series. For some reason, people love a series of paintings—perhaps they like comparing the various scenes. Whatever the reason, take advantage of it.

For example, you could do a watercolor of each church in your village, or within a ten- or fifteen-mile radius. If you have too many churches for the space available to you, display them in time segments, or a sequence.

Here's another successful series I did: You no doubt have seen posters with a montage of doors; I've even seen them with a montage of windows. For example, we have a poster in the Reading area called "The Doors of Reading." Well, we have doors in Hamburg too, not as many or as varied and fancy as a metropolitan area, but interesting just the same. Your area has them too—paint them just like I did, quarter sheet in a simple mat. People love them and had a great time identifying them. Also, a painting of someone's door could lead to a house painting...it did for me.

Use your imagination. Paint a series of red barns, or portraits of your town's leading citizens. An acquaintance told me of a store that displayed photographs of all the cats that lived in local shops, such as the bookstore and a cafe. Passersby pored over the photos trying to figure out which cat lived where. That idea could work as a series of paintings too!

A word of caution is necessary here. I have suggested that you paint series of similar subjects as attention getters and possible sales. Don't fall into the trap of painting solely for the purpose of sales. I happen to like to paint the churches and doors. You must paint for yourself, to your standards, your subject matter, your specialty.

The Geigers' Door,
11x7½ inches,
watercolor.

Borough Hall Door,
11x7½ inches,
watercolor.

Thomas Insurance Agency Door,
11x7½ inches,
watercolor.

Lizzie Neff Mansion Door,
11x7½ inches,
watercolor.

People are drawn to a series of similar paintings, particularly when they're displayed together. Doors make an interesting series because there is such variety. I paint these small door paintings because I like to do them, but they sell well because they cost less than a large watercolor. They also often lead to a commission for a house portrait.

I did a whole series on steeples— seventeen in all. A local merchant liked them, put them in his window, and ran a "Name the Steeple" contest. The contest attracted a lot of attention for the merchant and we sold all the paintings. (Note that not all the steeples were on churches. Buildings such as the library and fire company have steeples too!)

First United Church
of Christ Steeple,
14x11 inches,
watercolor.

Hamburg Public Library Steeple,
14x11 inches,
watercolor.

Bethany United Methodist
Church Steeple,
14x11 inches,
watercolor.

Union Fire Co. Steeple,
14x11 inches,
watercolor.

Ground Fog,
15x22 inches,
watercolor.

Moody paintings like this one of a barn in fog sometimes do well in mall sales because people respond to the mysterious feeling conveyed.

HAVE A CONTEST

Another great way to attract attention is to have a contest. It's a sure-fire method to get people interested in your work. Here's what I did: I was painting a series of church steeples. As I circulated through town gathering materials for my sketches, I realized that churches weren't the only buildings that had steeples. There were steeples on the fire hall, the library, and the borough hall. By the time I was finished I had seventeen very nice quarter-sheet watercolors of steeples within a five-mile radius.

I realized that while most people could easily recognize the facade of the church as a whole, isolating the steeple was something else again. It wasn't too easy to identify the steeple. I showed the paintings to a local merchant and he was so interested that he put them in his window and ran a *Name the Steeple* contest. He was delighted with the promotion and the interest it engendered. I was delighted too because I sold all seventeen of the paintings.

BE PATIENT

Don't expect overnight or sensational results. The only "instant" I've run into is instant coffee. It does take time for the word about your paintings to spread, but spread it will because people do check windows…and people do look… and people do talk and tell their friends…and I learned that people do buy. After the "series type" paintings (and even in between) I started to display some of my landscapes and townscapes and interest in them too started to develop.

As you progress you can start to promote that image you are beginning to create. Put a sign with your paintings pointing out that you accept commissions. Remind people that your paintings do become treasured gifts for birthdays, anniversaries, and the holidays. You may not be able to do that in some kind merchant's window, you must remember you are *in their space,* with their permission, so you don't want to create any competition for them. However, there is nothing to prevent you from tooting your own horn on your turf.

LOCAL ART AND CRAFT SHOWS

Every little town and area has them. I don't mean the mall shows, the regional and the juried shows; we'll touch on them later. I am referring to the small non-juried local shows both indoor and outdoor that are sponsored by local churches, fire companies, and service clubs. Sometimes they are used as fund-raisers but mostly as a showcase for the talents of their members and friends.

By all means participate in these. You can't get any closer to the grass roots than this because you are displaying your artwork, which is local in subject matter, to local people, many of whom will tell you, "I didn't know you were doing anything like this." They will also tell you, "I didn't know our little community could be so beautiful."

If your area doesn't have an arts and crafts show, then consider having one; organize one and have your church, club, or group sponsor it. The main thrust may have to be on crafts rather than art, because there may not be too many artists like yourself around. But you'd be surprised—there are more expressions of talent going on in your area than you realize. Uncover it! Get the artists together and have a show! Why? To promote participation in arts and crafts, to get more people involved in expressing themselves in some form of artistic endeavor. If you do this honestly then sales will ultimately come.

Timing is helpful. Late October and early November are good show times because that time of the year finds people in a buying mood because of the approaching holiday season.

Solar Tea,
15x22 inches,
watercolor.

Be sure to include a variety of paintings in any sidewalk or mall show. For me, still lifes like this one provide a pleasant change from village scenes and landscapes.

MALL AND SIDEWALK SALES

After participating in your smaller local arts and crafts shows held by the service clubs, fire companies, churches, and so forth, you may want to spread out a bit more. As you develop and mature you should keep an eye on the larger shows beyond your area. Let's call them regional shows. These shows are held in enclosed malls, in shady parks and recreation areas, on the busy downtown sidewalks, on the sunny shoreline boardwalks, and in some cases on blocked-off streets in the business sections of larger towns and cities.

You might want to limit yourself to shows taking place within an eighty- to one-hundred-mile radius of your home. You could use a two-hour driving trip as your range. Anything further than that might require an overnight stay in order to arrive, set up, and be open for business by 9 A.M. Remember the same time constraints apply to the break-down period at the end of the show, which is usually around 9 P.M.

The classified sections of the art magazines usually list these shows state by state. Write to those within your range and obtain the rules for exhibition, costs, etc. Before you jump in, visit as many as you can; talk to exhibitors, compare their work to yours, get a feel for what takes place and learn as much as you can. Artists are usually the friendliest of people and are most willing to share information and exchange ideas; after all, this is how they got started.

Study the wide variety of display units and display bins that are used to mount and show paintings, both those that are framed and those that are only matted. Pay particular attention to the provisions for providing quick cover in case of sudden rain showers and sudden wind storms. Play a little mental game; pick out a display booth that is attractive to you. Now step back and take it apart and put it together to see if you can anticipate any weaknesses it may have.

Speak to the artists and seek their counsel; tell them you are a rookie seeking information. You'll be amazed at how receptive they are to your questions and how helpful they are with their answers. They will gladly tell you how they got started and give you suppliers' names and addresses. Now you must be prepared to accept that all groups have their stinkers, and artists do too, but don't let that very, very small minority affect your enthusiasm.

Your homework isn't completed without a study of the smaller details. Tedious as they may be, these details are most important and I'll list a few of them:

■ How does your work compare to those exhibited, both in quality and pricing?

■ How are the prices shown on the paintings? Pick out the style you like.

■ Compare various mat and frame styles—you'll be surprised at the assortment.

■ Check all the paintings from an artistic viewpoint. You'll be amazed at the wide variety of styles, designs, and moods in which subjects are painted. You'll find hundreds of ideas you can use in the future.

■ Take a small notebook along (memo size) and make notes in your own "artistic shorthand" of the ideas that intrigue you.

■ Watch a sale being made. Do they use a bill of sale? How is the sold painting transferred from artist to buyer—wrapped, bagged, what style?

■ And this is important: Where does the artist put the check or cash they received? A tin box or a pouch on their person? Where? Does the artist replace that painting with another? Where did they get it? Where do they keep their extra stock?

■ Can you find the artist at each booth? Look for them. Sometimes they are sitting in or by the booth. Sometimes they are sketching. Often the booth looks unattended, but it really isn't. The artist may be in the midway or aisle listening to viewers' comments, or darting in and out to provide comments of their own.

Your first show of this kind is the toughest one because you feel so vulnerable, so alone. But relax, it isn't that tough at all. It is a good way to banter with people and listen to the browsers' comments and reactions to your work. It is a good training experience for learning how to deal with the public. I exhibit in this fashion three to four times a year, always with a moderate measure of success (enough to want to continue on this limited basis) but there are artists who travel far and wide exhibiting in mall and sidewalk shows only, because they find them to be very financially rewarding—their only source of income—and they like to do them. You won't know if it is for you unless you try.

In for Repairs,
by Tony Couch,
15x22 inches,
watercolor.

Tony Couch is a master at incorporating all the principles of design into each of his watercolors and that is why his paintings usually are accepted by juries when he chooses to exhibit.

WHAT ABOUT THOSE JURIED EXHIBITS?

Whether you should enter juried exhibits depends upon what you are searching for... sales or acclaim. It certainly is very gratifying to have one or two paintings accepted for display in a regional or national exhibition and provides a tremendous boost to the ego when you can list these acceptances in your résumé. Your ultimate goal or objective may be achieved more quickly if your dossier lists a large number of acceptances.

However, there is a price you may have to pay. Your attitude must be stoic because you aren't going to be accepted by every exhibit; in fact it may be a long time until you are accepted at all...and sometimes that hurts. You are at the mercy of the juror. You spent hours planning and ultimately executing your masterpiece and in just moments (sometimes seconds) the juror rejects it. You must be prepared to accept this. Sometimes they are polite and send notices that say "not accepted" instead of "rejected." Either way it still hurts.

In addition you must remember that these are really just exhibitions. The public, the jurors, the media critics, and the society sponsoring the exhibit look upon it as a free display of talent. Oh yes, the paintings are for sale; the brochure says so, but there is no sales effort and the number that is actually sold is pathetically few, possibly one or two per hundred. I used to enter quite a lot of them and was lucky enough to have some work accepted, but now I am very selective as to which exhibitions I will attempt to enter. You and you alone must be the

judge as to whether you want to get involved.

Having said all that, let's look at what is involved.

The classified sections of the art magazines list the competitions that are available and usually list them by state. They also include listings of gallery shows as well as fairs and festivals. Ninety-five percent of them are juried by slides. It would be well worth your time to make a list of shows and competitions that interest you and send for the prospectus, which lists and describes the jurors plus all other entry information. This will give you a feel for the rules and regulations. The instructions are usually quite complete, and will inform you about size and framing limitations, the type of medium the show will accept, as well as deadlines.

What Do Jurors Look For?

Obviously your paintings will have to be good works of art but that isn't enough; there are other areas that will need your attention, too.

Matting and Framing—Surprisingly, a painting is often rejected because the framing isn't appropriate. It may overpower the painting when its real function is to support or complement the work of art.

Photography—Usually the jurors will view a slide of your entry so you not only must produce a good work of art but also a good slide of it. Some artists have a professional photographer produce the slide. If you want to do your own photographic work, use a camera with a single-lens reflex viewfinder. This will permit

Pig Iron, Sand and Coke,
22x30 inches,
watercolor.
Collection of Mr. and Mrs. Carl A. Francis.

This painting seemed to have what juries were looking for since it was accepted in a number of shows. However, there is no exact science to jurying because sometimes a painting is accepted by one jury and passed over by the next. You must learn to accept these differences of opinion by juries—the buying public is the ultimate juror.

you to fill the viewing frame with your painting only and eliminate extraneous material. What you see is what you get. An SLR camera also will help you produce sharp focus and proper exposure. (See Chapter 8 for more on photographing your artwork.)

It is very difficult to pinpoint in each show's case just what the jurors like and dislike, what they will and won't accept, but through the years I think I have learned about some dos and don'ts and I will list them here:

■ Jurors seem to favor correct value patterns as well as good design; they like paintings that make a statement such as mood or special character; good execution appeals to them and new approaches seem to gain acceptance.

■ Jurors do not seem to favor the usual clichés: sand dunes, gull over breaking waves, seascapes, the usual snow scenes, barns and more barns, flowers, and vignettes. They do seem to be attracted (for the time being at least) to semi-abstracts and semi-avant-garde paintings. This phase will change in time, too.

■ Don't "paint for a juror." If you know that a juror likes to paint baskets and bottles,

don't try to win favor by entering a painting of similar subject matter. That juror will be very critical of your efforts.

■ Your work should have *immediate visual impact*. It must "carry across the room." Let me explain. The jurors may have to look at possibly 300 to 400 slide entries, even 800 to 900 is not unusual. If we suppose that they view just 300 slides for ten seconds each, it will take five hours for just the first look. So in order to conserve time the jurors may hurry the first screening and that first quick look at your slide may last just five seconds, or even less. From this you can see that your painting should have some immediate wallop. At least this approach will receive a closer look than a painting with subtle values and delicate color changes.

If a painting isn't accepted, I think of it as "passed by" by the judges. I abhor the use of the word rejected in the art world. Webster defines reject this way: "to discard or throw out as worthless, useless, or substandard." Always remember when you receive a rejection notice that your work is not worthless, or useless, or substandard. That particular juror may reject your work in

only four seconds but that doesn't mean the painting is worthless or useless. You liked it and other people like it, too. Treat your entries into regional and national juried shows as educational experiences. It is great if your pieces are accepted and if you win awards, but if you don't, get over the hurt quickly. Don't waste any time shedding big tears.

I am more satisfied with my achievement when the person in the street puts a check in my hand for a painting that they want and like than when a couple of jurors point thumbs up and say, "The exhibition will now show your painting."

I am not downgrading juried shows, they are important, but don't take the black pill if it seems forever before you are accepted. They are, however, one of the best ways to grow as an artist because you should set your sights on acceptance in a specific area or regional show. When you have reached that plateau, then you can upgrade your goals to more prestigious shows and compete with artists at that level. The extra work and effort that you expend to achieve these goals are bound to show up as improvement in your artistic expertise.

Russell Steel

Russell Steel is an artist whose work has received wide recognition, but who still chooses to paint small, simple sketches that are popular in his hometown.

Russell is a signatory member of the Southwestern Watercolor Society in Dallas and has exhibited in Watercolor West, New Mexico Small Paintings, and the International Watercolor Show in New Orleans, as well as one traveling show of the AWS.

Yet more often than not you'll find Russell at his easel on the sidewalks of Durango, Colorado, where he lives. Durango has many tourist attractions, such as the Durango to Silverton Railroad and the historic Strater Hotel. He paints simple ink line and wash watercolors that have proven to be very popular with tourists to the area.

Russell and his wife, Audrey, also own and operate the Cinders Gallery on Main Street, a half block from the Durango Narrow Gauge Railroad Station, which serves as an outlet for his paintings.

Choosing to paint scenes in a small town and paint them in a way that is popular with tourists doesn't prostitute Russell's creativity. The watercolors are lovely loose sketches Russell enjoys painting. They bring pleasure and beauty to those who buy them, and at the same time create a cash flow that allows Russell to devote time to painting other subjects. Everyone's a winner in this situation, and you can do it too.

Russell Steel and his wife operate their own gallery in Durango's downtown area. The gallery provides a perfect outlet for the type of paintings Steel does, which appeal to locals and tourists alike.

Hotel Strater, Durango, Colorado, by Russell Steel, 14x11 inches, ink line and wash.

Narrow Gauge, by Russell Steel, 11x14 inches, ink line and wash.

ARRANGE YOUR OWN ONE-ARTIST SHOW

You might consider mounting a show of your work in your own community once a year. This would serve several purposes. Even though you have been selling your work, this show would focus attention on new work, you would get additional people exposed to that new work, you'll get more publicity and even increased sales.

I have a friend who mounts her own one-artist show periodically in her home. She has compiled a special invitation list from past clients, possible new clients, coworkers, and special friends, to name a few. The shows are very successful because she conducts them with great taste, special tact, and marvelous watercolors.

It needn't cost an "arm and a leg" to do it. With some careful planning and ingenuity you should be able to keep your expenses to your level. The key word here is *planning:*

1. An ideal time is late October or early November (when the banks distribute their Christmas Club checks).

2. Locate an empty store front in an area that has both pedestrian and vehicular traffic. In today's volatile retail climate that shouldn't be too difficult.

3. Compile a mailing list for announcements or invitations, and design and hand letter them yourself. (You are an artist, aren't you?) These can be printed offset instead of typeset and can also be reproduced by photocopy machine. Design them in such a fashion that they can be used as handbills, too. They can be distributed in many ways in addition to mail: store counters, bulletin boards, parking lots.

4. *You must let the public know about it!* Get a feature story with some photographs into the local newspaper, even if it is a weekly. Don't overlook your local cable TV company. Most have one channel that is used for local classified-type advertising (along with time and weather checks) and the cost is very reasonable. Use your supermarket bulletin boards; almost all stores have them now. Use the announcements as window posters, or use them as the foundation for larger posters for windows.

The number of paintings you should hang for your show depends on your individual situation. Hang as many as you have room for and can still hang in good taste. Let the variety be representative of the work you are producing. All pieces should be priced; let the viewer know up front what the price is. (This delicate area is discussed thoroughly in Chapter 9.)

You may not want to mount a show such as this and be the sole sponsor. This should not deter you; have a friend be your sponsor and let that person be your patron and present your work in your home, in their home, in rented spaces, or in whatever spaces you have available.

These suggestions are just that...suggestions. They are meant to start your creative wheels turning. You will succeed if your exhibit is in a place where people can easily see it and get to it; it will succeed if you tell as many people as you can about it; it will succeed if you put prices on your paintings that will permit viewers to buy the one they want.

Approaching Storm at Sutliff's,
by Mary Keiser,
19¼x26¼ inches,
watercolor.

Mary Keiser has a unique way of marketing her watercolors. At this stage of her development she has been selling all of her production by mounting her own one-artist shows periodically in her own home.

SET UP A GALLERY IN YOUR HOME

If there is a gallery in your locality and if it is receptive to exhibiting and promoting your paintings, then by all means use it. (You should also have a gallery connection that is some distance from your home area.) If there is no gallery in your locality then establish one…in your home.

Before we go too far here, I think we must clarify the word *gallery*. What I really mean is a space where someone can view your work, not a commercial gallery that promotes and sells all types of artwork. You don't have to set up a gallery with reception area, unusual lighting for walls designed to show many paintings, special browsing racks, and display units.

People often tell me they would like to see my work. It is rather awkward to refer them to a commercial gallery in the next city some miles distant. So I developed display space in my home where I could show my work to interested people, be it friends or even prospective clients. My gallery is by appointment only, very low key, one client at a time. The neighborhood is not disturbed by commercial traffic or parking problems; there is no violation of zoning regulations or business codes. If you opt to go this route too, it would be good to check these regulations in your area. The local zoning officer in your community can help you with these regulations. There is no special telephone listing and no exterior sign or shingle. Do I sell in this atmosphere? Certainly I do, and so will you!

It would be ideal if you could use one of the rooms in your house for a gallery, and gallery only, preferably next to your studio or work space. Your family status and home size will determine this, but rarely is this extra space available. I'm fortunate enough to have such a space available next to my studio, but it is on my third floor. It is as close to heaven as I'll get with complete isolation, no street noises, no house noises or distractions. However, receiving the general public there is impractical and quite an invasion of privacy, so I opted to use the living room. At first this sounds like quite an invasion of privacy too, but consider this: You do not have clients coming and going *every day* and not at those odd and unusual hours. Most visits are by invitation and you must remember it is the living room that usually is in best shape to receive someone on the spur of the moment.

Waiting for the Buffalo, 11x15 inches, watercolor.

This is the type of painting that sells well from my home gallery. A variation on the "Pennsylvania Railroad Station" on page 46, this painting shows the station in a different mood. People used to wait for the last train, the 9:15 to Buffalo, in the dark. They didn't call it "the 9:15"; instead, they called it "the Buffalo." Townsfolk who remember those days love paintings from that era.

You too can do this if you hang as many of your paintings on the walls as good taste will allow (and do rotate them). Buy a good sturdy portable art rack that will hold thirty or forty pieces of your work (some even hold fifty, or at least that is what their advertising says). Racks of this nature are easy to make but I opted to buy one; I didn't want that home-made look in the living room. Place it in a corner of the living room so that it is out of the daily traffic patterns. When a client arrives, and this is usually by invitation or appointment, I set up a conventional card table so that paintings can be perused in the rack, or they can be removed, handled, or stacked on the table.

This set-up provides clients with some flexibility. They can sit on the sofa and view any paintings they are interested in when I place them on the opposing wall, they can handle them at arm's length, stack them, or whatever. All paintings except the framed ones on the wall are mounted on foam-core board, matted, and shrink-wrapped. (More on this later.) I have found this system to work very well.

CONSIDER THIS GIVE-AWAY

One great way to build your image is to give potential customers a little piece of art to remember you by. I've found an illustrated bookmark to be greatly appreciated. You can give them to the president of a club where you've spoken, to a customer who visits your home gallery, to anyone you'd like to have think of you.

■ Take scraps of mat board and cut them into strips 2x7 inches (you can vary the size to your taste). You can also use 140-pound or 300-pound watercolor paper.

■ Paint a small, simple yet colorful design on it.
■ Punch a hole in the top portion. Now take some colorful yarn and thread it through the hole.

Voilà! The recipients are delighted for here is something petite and personal that they can enjoy every time they read. You can even put a personal message on the top bare space. Create your own design.

Note: This is not my personal creation; I've seen them at show booths from time to time (some artists even create them for sale). I make them as give-aways and they are received with great appreciation.

A give-away like these bookmarks is a terrific way to build good will. You can give them to potential customers at shows, sidewalk sales, your home gallery—they'll remember you kindly.

The Emhardt Home,
15x22 inches,
watercolor.
Courtesy of Mr. and Mrs.
Edward Emhardt.

When you set up a gallery or display area in your home, be sure to have examples on hand of good reproductions in color print form or colored slide to show a visitor or client what can be done. Not every home is an architectural gem or artistically exciting. But it is possible to produce a pleasant image of a "plain jane," too. All a client is looking for is a fair illustration of their home…with a little artistic license on the side.

Schonour Home,
15x22 inches,
watercolor.
Collection of
Randolph and Pamela Schonour.

Cranford Home,
15x22 inches,
watercolor.
Collection of
Ronald and Patricia Cranford.

CHAPTER 7

Delivering your paintings

■ You have just finished a watercolor. You spent many hours on its design, made a number of value sketches, and devoted a considerable amount of time to its execution in final form. You like it—it's pretty good! What happens next is equally important. You want to present that watercolor in a favorable way; your presentation must support and complement the painting.

One of the decisions you must make is what to do about mats and frames. There are three approaches to handling a finished watercolor. First, you can do nothing to it—no mat, no frame—just store it flat and put it in a simple temporary mat when a client wants to look at it. Second, you can mount it on a backing piece of foam board and cover it with a mat and shrink-wrapping, and it will still be fairly simple to store. Third, you can frame it or have it framed by a professional framer, ready to wall-mount. There is merit to all three procedures so let's discuss them in depth.

NO MAT, NO FRAME

Some artists do just this. No mat and no frame and I guess they do it because of lack of space and for ease of handling. I have a friend who paints only on full sheets (22x30 inches) and he carries quite a few of these with him as he makes calls on prospective clients. When he makes a presentation he places each painting in a temporary trial viewing mat (as illustrated in Chapter 2) as it is individually reviewed.

Another friend puts a ½-inch strip of masking tape around each edge of her watercolors. After the piece is finished she removes the masking tape and this leaves a ½-inch white border around the watercolor and gives it a "sort of mat look."

In both instances the reasons they handle their work in this manner are lack of storage space and the desire to cut weight as they transport their work. One of them does a bit of flying so the reduced weight is an advantage.

I first painted this at half-sheet size. I liked it but felt it would be better in full-sheet size, so I re-painted the scene. The owner knew I was painting the mill and asked to see the results, so I showed him both paintings. He and his wife bought both, the larger one for themselves and the original for a daughter. If I'd shown the owner only the "final product," I would have lost a sale.

Milling Since 1772,
21x29 inches,
watercolor.
Collection of Mr. and Mrs. Donald Anthony.

SIMPLE MAT AND WRAP

You will be handling your matted pieces, putting them in and out of storage, showing them, reviewing them, and in addition to all of that your clients will also want to handle them, so they should be protected in some fashion. I have devised a system that requires me to cut my mats only about 20 percent of the time. I have standardized my print sizes to eighth sheets (7x9 inches), quarter sheets (11x15 inches), half sheets (15x22 inches), and full sheets (22x30 inches). This permits me to buy three uniform size bevel mats from a commercial supplier:

■ ⅛ sheet — 11x14-inch beveled mat with 8x9-inch opening

■ ¼ sheet — 16x20-inch beveled mat with 10x14-inch opening

■ ½ sheet — 22x28-inch beveled mat with 14x20-inch opening

When I need the fourth size (full sheet) I cut these myself: 28x36-inch beveled mat with 21x29-inch opening.

The standard mats feature professional hand-cut beveled edges and pH neutral stock. By buying only three uniform sizes, I reduce my inventory and costs. I purchase them by mail; there are a number of specialty houses and framing supply houses that furnish mats in this fashion. I located my source in the classified section of one of the art magazines.

For a mounting board I use foam board (some suppliers call it Fome-Cor Board), which I buy from the same vendor that supplies me with uniform cut mats. Foam board is a virtually weightless board made of polystyrene foam core laminated on both sides with a white coated paper stock. It makes a very strong, stiff back-up for framed work and a great mounting board for watercolor paintings, posters, etc. It cuts easily with a mat knife to frame size. I purchase it in sheet size 22x28 inches.

Let's assume we have completed a half-sheet watercolor and want to prepare it for delivery. When I laid out the sketch on the 15x22-inch Arches paper, I laid out the image size to 15x21 inches because the opening on the mat will be 14x20.

Here's what to do:

1. Cut a piece of foam board to 22x28 inches.

2. Mount the watercolor centered on the foam board with one-inch gummed linen tape. Put a strip 1x3 inches long along the top edge, one strip on each side. This tape is neutral pH, white, and used for repairs and reinforcing.

3. Place your 22x28-inch mat on top of it.

Old Courthouse, Newcastle, Delaware
by John Wenger,
6x6 inches,
watercolor.

If you don't want to shrink-wrap your paintings, here's another way to protect them. John Wenger places watercolors like this one in a simple mat and then inserts the matted painting in a clear polyethylene envelope. These envelopes are available in fifty different sizes and their cost is reasonable. Check the advertisements in artists' magazines for suppliers.

If you are going to frame your watercolor, this sandwich is now ready for your framing procedure. I'll explain that in the framing section.

If you are not going to frame it immediately, then wrap this sandwich with shrink-wrap film. Shrink-wrap is acid free, fifty-gauge clear film and supplied by most of the large artist supply houses. I buy it in a roll thirty-six inches wide and five hundred feet long, for approximately $48. I know this sounds like a lot of money, and it is, but there is enough material on the roll to wrap approximately 150 half-sheet size watercolors. Not all of your watercolors will be half-sheet size, some will be smaller, so the average unit cost will be reduced to approximately 30 cents per watercolor and that is a small price to pay for the protection it affords.

Shrink-wrap is a great system for the protection of artwork while on temporary display. You can purchase a shrink-wrap machine from many mail-order suppliers. It contains a specialty shelf for the shrink-wrap film. The film is pulled over the mounted and matted artwork and overlapped on the back. Then the heating elements are applied to the back and the heat makes the film shrink and seal itself. The cost of a shrink-wrap machine ranges between $200 to $300 depending upon the model and the vendor.

You can shrink-wrap your artwork yourself by using a hair dryer; a couple of experimental wraps as a trial run and the whole procedure is perfected. Here is how you do it. Diaper wrap your material; the ends of the shrink-wrap can be taped to the back of the material. Use a 1,200 watt or 1,500 watt hair dryer to tighten the shrink-wrap around the painting. This is the method I use and the shrink-wrap gets as tight as a drum.

There is another method. Diaper your material, overlapping the shrink-wrap on the back, then using a household iron set to the permanent press setting and a piece of kraft paper between the iron and the shrink-wrap, press down with the edge of the iron on the overlapped areas to seal them. After sealing the shrink-wrap to itself, the iron can be used to iron both sides, using kraft paper between, to shrink the wrap. *Do not at any time allow the iron to come in direct contact with the shrink-wrap* because it will melt under direct heat. Always use paper between the iron and shrink-wrap. The heat setting on the iron should be adjusted as necessary.

You now have a painting that can be handled without fear of dust, dirt, or any other smudge. As you show paintings to your clients in your gallery in your home (Chapter 6), you can stand them on edge against a chair, or on an easel or counter for viewing and admiration.

Also, clients can take a painting home and handle it while they move it from place to place, room to room, and wall to wall until they decide where they want to put it and how they want it framed. Many times clients like to make their own frames in their own shop. Fine. All they have to do is remove the shrink-wrap; the watercolor is already mounted and matted, ready for framing.

A word of caution about shrink-wrap. I treat all the salable pieces (that are not framed) in shrink-wrap fashion on a backboard of foam board. There is this one disadvantage though: Since the foam board back is $3/16$-inch thick you may have some storage problems. You can stack about three times as many watercolors without foam board backs in the space needed for those using the foam board backing.

But the benefits far outweigh the disadvantages. The concern for soil and smudges is diminished. In my home gallery I find clients like to pick up a piece and hold it at arm's length to look at it. Then they will set it on the telly or the sofa, or a chair for a ten-foot look…and curiously that slight bit of reflection that you get at times helps the painting.

FRAMING

Sometimes the decision to frame or not to frame will depend upon the level of achievement you've reached. If your paintings have reached the point where you can price them *(and sell them)* at let's say the $1,000 to $2,500 range, then by all means have them framed by a professional framer. The cost of the framing will not represent a large percentage of your selling price.

However, if your paintings are in the $150 to $500 range, the additional price of the framing could alter the final price considerably. It could raise the price higher than a customer wants (or is able) to pay. I've sold paintings to clients who in turn took them to a framer and wound up paying as much for the framing as they did for the artwork in the first place. (Ironically, this disparity doesn't hurt you the artist that much because the client now realizes that he or she got a pretty good deal from you pricewise.) But most

of my customers aren't prepared to pay as much for framing as they paid for the artwork itself.

I am not discrediting the professional framer. The good ones are professionals, too, who can take a good watercolor and give it an *elegant* appearance. They will mat it in appropriate single, double, or triple style of the proper colors, then place it in a suitable frame and the result will be a very tasteful piece of art. The professional framer has a business to run that requires a lot of stock on hand as well as expertise, and is entitled to a fair profit. But sometimes professional framing is not appropriate because it costs more than the customer can or will pay.

The decisions about framing are personal ones and should be made not by you, but by the buyer. When I am discussing a commission with a client we usually review framing. Sometimes they have strong feelings about it because they prefer a certain type of frame, wood or steel, and a particular mat style. They have

a particular place where this painting will be hung and it must be coordinated. In cases such as this I will deliver the completed work simply mounted and matted.

Conversely, the client many times will tell me to frame the painting. I don't want to sell framing—I want to sell my watercolors, so I keep my framing efforts very simple and not time consuming. In addition I strive to keep the cost as low as possible so that it will not balloon the cost of the artwork.

My theory is that the work of art is the star, the mat and frame are the supporting players, bit players. You should not even realize they are there. Consequently, my pieces are matted and framed very simply. When I do frame a painting for a client I use aluminum frame sections since they are available in a whole host of colors and contours. Instead of glass I use Plexiglas clear acrylic, which is a lightweight glazing material that has superior impact strength compared to glass. Its thickness of 0.125 inch is strong enough for

For John's Wife,
15x22 inches,
watercolor.
Courtesy of Mr. and Mrs. John C. Driscoll.

When this client and I discussed matting and framing, he asked that the finished watercolor not be framed. Because the painting was going to be placed in a dining room furnished with cherry furniture and he is a partner in a furniture business, he opted to make the matching frame himself.

frames holding full-sheet watercolors in 30x36-inch aluminum frames.

All of this, the mounting foam board, the mat, the frame, and the acrylic glaze is still a low-cost package that will not upset the pricing of the watercolor by too large a percentage; at least it doesn't double the total cost. I find that if I sell a watercolor for $200 and do my own simple framing I'll add $50 and clients accept this price. If they go to a professional framer they may pay $125 to $175 for the frame. In any event, when the billing is made up I always list the price of the watercolor and the price of the framing separately rather than in one lump sum. But, more about pricing in Chapter 9.

I must hasten to add though, as you progress (and I am still growing), once in a while you produce a real gem—a *classic!* When that happens to me, then I have that classic matted and framed by a professional framer before I offer it for sale. It's worth the extra expense to give your best work the best possible framing job.

Christ Church, Niantic,
1836-1872,
21x27 inches,
watercolor.
Courtesy of
Mr. and Mrs. Ronald Cranford.

When Christ Church of Niantic, Pennsylvania, celebrated its 150th anniversary, a committee of parishioners asked me to produce a watercolor of their second church building. They didn't have any photographs, but they did have a copy of the architect's written specifications, translated from German to English, that were quite detailed. In addition to preliminary value sketches, I made several quarter-sheet color studies that were complete paintings in themselves. The committee members were so pleased they bought all the color sketches.

SOMETHING DIFFERENT

When you've finished a painting and gotten it ready to deliver to the customer or to show in your home gallery, you'll want to add a name card that gives your name, address, telephone number, and other pertinent information. You can also use name cards to give the title or price of a painting in a show, hand out to browsers at art fairs, enclose in correspondence, and for dozens of other uses.

Because I use a name card in so many ways, its design had to be simple. I also wanted to confine myself to one color of ink to keep costs down, but I wanted a card that was both professional and artistic looking. You can see the end result at right.

The blank white space at the top of the card can be used to write in the price, message, or whatever.

Reverse printing gives the card a two-color effect. To add more color, I take a brush, charge it with a color(or even two), and make a quick pass across the card. I do it by laying out a large quantity of cards on the drawing board at one time, and it only takes a moment to do the whole lot. It's quick, easy, and has a bright, eye-catching look that would cost far more to have printed.

An attractive name card is a nice finishing touch. I keep costs down by printing my cards with just one color of ink and adding a splash of additional color with my brush.

Anthony-Antanavage House, Circa 1919,
15x22 inches,
watercolor.

*I delivered this painting framed,
and the owners were so pleased
with it they invited friends and
neighbors for a party to celebrate
the hanging.*

In Our Second Century,
15x11 inches,
watercolor.
Collection of
Burkey and Driscoll.

*The highs and lows of these
storefronts attracted me to this
scene, which I painted on a
quarter sheet and matted but did
not frame. The owners of one of the
businesses, a funeral home and
furniture store that dates back to
around 1820, bought the painting
and have since commissioned other
pieces.*

CHAPTER 8

Keeping the books

■ While the keeping of your business records is a personal matter, I do believe it would be worthwhile for us to discuss a few simple records that should be maintained. I know that your business probably isn't terribly complicated and that many of your transactions may be with friends and acquaintances, but even so it's important that those transactions be handled professionally.

BOOKKEEPING

I won't try to cover everything about bookkeeping, but will discuss briefly the basic records you should keep.

The supplies you'll need are simple. An inexpensive three-ring binder filled with ruled sheets will be adequate for most people. You can convert those horizontal ruled sheets to a columnar journal by hand ruling the number of columns you need, and separate the categories with tabbed dividers.

There are also a number of standard bookkeeping systems available for small businesses, such as the *Ideal Bookkeeping* series. You should review these. Basically, they are a one-binder system that has all the forms needed to record your sales, expenses, depreciations, etc. They are quite complete and not too expensive.

You may need a few other forms, such as bills of sale and large envelopes or files for keeping receipts, but nothing that's complicated or expensive.

Let's review the records you'll need to keep.

DATE	CHECK	CASH	ITEM	TOTAL	BREAK DOWN					
					ADV. (6)	CAR EXP. (9)	DUES & PUB. (13)	OFFICE EXPENSES (20)	Supplies (24)	MISC.
8.10.88		✓	copies at Bellevue	3.00				3.00		
8.15.88	✓		The Artist - Renewal	18.00			18.00			
8.15.88	✓		ASW - (1) Quire 140# Arches	76.15					76.15	
			ASW - 10 Tubes paint	24.67					24.67	
8.30.88	✓		Bell Toll - Studio Phone	17.48					Utilities	17.48
8.30.88		✓	Clausen Supplies - Staple	4.50				4.50		
		✓	Dana Advt - Flyers	19.75	19.75					
8.26.88		✓	Trip to Phila to Sawitt Gallery							
			150 mi × 24¢	36.00		36 —				
		✓	Meals in Phila	10.25					Travel	10.25
9.3.88		✓	Dick Blick Brush	10.50					10.50	
			Masket	3.50					3.50	
9.3.88		✓	Trip To Phila - Sawitt Gallery							
			150 mi @ 24¢	36.00		36 —				

Keep a record of all your expenses. Your records don't have to be complicated, as you can see from this sample, but should record the date, whether you paid by check or cash, the item and amount. I also record which category of deduction the expense falls under, using a system based on the IRS form, Schedule C.

Bill of Sale

When you make a sale it is always advisable to give the customer a bill of sale on which you record date of sale; buyer's name and address; item sold with description, price, manner of payment, and any special comments. This seems like a chore but it really isn't. Every stationery store has simple sales books (I like the no-carbon-required type) and each book has at least fifty duplicate sets of sales sheets. There is even room at the top where you can paste your return address label. Your clients deserve a receipt for the good money they are paying you.

This bill of sale is also very important to you because this is a part of your record of what you have sold. This sales information is transferred to a sales journal sheet described below.

Record of Sales

Transferring the information from the bill of sale to a record of sales allows you to keep all the vital information about your sales and clients in one place—as your sales grow, so will the reasons for keeping such a record.

I transfer the information on each bill of sale to a larger journal sheet in my three-ring binder, where I can keep a running total on "sales to date." This assembles the information from twenty or twenty-five bills of sale onto one easy-to-read journal sheet, thereby making it much easier to check past transactions. Since you are selling a product, your sales will have to be listed as income on your tax returns and this record makes that easy to do.

Record of Expenditures

While you are creating and selling, you will also generate expenses that can be used as deductions to offset income on your tax returns. That's why keeping a record of expenditures is important.

You must get in the habit of obtaining receipts for all of your purchases and expenditures, and I emphasize ALL! Get in the habit of saving all cash register receipts, even for those "little items" that seem insignificant, because those small items can nickel and dime you to death. They add up to dollars very quickly. At the end of the month, sort them out and record them on an Expense Sheet. Rule this sheet with as many columns for breakdowns as you feel you'll need and keep it in the back half of that three-ring binder you bought. Your larger purchases can be made by check, and you can record them in the expense record.

Let's pause here for a moment. You'll simplify things for yourself greatly if you do not co-mingle your art receipts and art expenditures in your personal checking account. As your sales and expenditures increase, open a separate account. By the time you reach this point you'll do well to seek the advice of an accountant, or at least review it with the person who prepares your tax returns, who can advise you as to what expenses you can or cannot deduct and what records you must maintain.

Before you begin to lay out and rule your expense sheets into columns you would do well to obtain a copy of the IRS form, Schedule C: Profit or (Loss) from Business or Profession. You will be required to file this form with your tax return if you operate your artistic endeavor as a business and not a hobby. You can't operate a hobby at a loss and use those losses to offset other income you have. But if your art has shown a profit in three out of five years, you may be able to establish it as a business. As such, you may be able to use the losses in the two unprofitable years to offset other income.

The burden of proof will be yours. You must prove to the IRS that you really and truly had a profit motive even when you did not make a profit—that you are indeed conducting your art as a business and are trying to make a profit. In order to do this, you will have to maintain complete records.

You would do well to review this with an accountant or your tax preparer. Also, the IRS has a free publication that can help, *Publication 334, Tax Guide for Small Business,* and book stores have a number of books and guides devoted to taxes.

I used Schedule C to set up the deductions portion of my records. I ruled my paper into seven columns and used those columns to record the expenses that I incur most frequently. I gave each column a heading and also recorded the line number used on Schedule C for that deduction. For example, I have columns headed "Advertising (6)," "Dues and Publications (13)," and "Office Expenses (20)." (I made one copy of the ruled sheets and then photocopied it to provide all the blank forms I'd need. Once you get your system under control, you can have forms printed or use standard forms.)

Once again, I do urge you to review your system with, or have your system devised by, an accountant or your tax preparer. This person will give you the proper advice needed to record and substantiate your deductions.

Taxes and Licenses

As a selling artist you now have other responsibilities in addition to your federal and state income tax. You also may be required to collect a sales tax for the state in which you do business and possibly a sales tax at the county or local level too. Seek the advice of an accountant, your tax preparer, or obtain the information and instructions from your state tax office. The state tax office will issue a permit to collect the state sales tax and this permit will have an identifying number that you will have to display and also use when filing your returns. The state will also issue instructions about calculating the tax, collecting it, and transmitting it to the collection office. It is really a simple procedure.

Your local area governments (county, township, or borough) may also require a business license, permit, and they may even have a mercantile tax of some sort. A visit to your local area government office will clarify these possibilities for you.

The Dunkle House,
1938-1972,
15x22 inches,
watercolor.
Courtesy of Mr. and Mrs. Paul Dunkle.

This painting is a typical anniversary gift. This couple moved to New Mexico in 1972, and their children commissioned this painting of their home in Hamburg for their 50th wedding anniversary. All of this information is recorded on the art sold file card like the one shown on the next page.

RECORD-KEEPING

While bookkeeping is necessary to your financial well being, record-keeping is just as important to your artistic progress. There is a cliché that artists are notoriously poor business people. I'm not too sure that I agree with this platitude. Record-keeping requires a little discipline and this is a trait you can easily develop. Below I'll outline some of the records you should consider keeping and why you'll find them useful.

Art Log
You bought a three-ring binder and filled it with compositional ruled paper for your record of sales. Now buy a simple set of indexes (tabbed pages). Use one section for sales, one section for expenditures, and use one section for an art log. Record in chrono-logical order every show you enter and comments pertinent thereto. In addition record every painting that you place, display, or loan, and the date. Be sure to record the dates those paintings were returned as well as any pertinent comments (and record if the piece was accepted in that show). Believe it or not, without an art log you'll lose track of what paintings are where and just which shows you entered after you've been at it for a while.

Art Sold Bin
The most important record I maintain is my art sold bin because I refer to it time and time again. It provides me with important information about what I've sold, to whom, for how much, and what the response was.

It also serves as a mini-portfolio that can be useful when talking to potential buy-ers. When I discuss a commission or a sale with a client, sometimes we look through the art sold bin for ideas, for comparisons, or whatever. I spend more time on this record than any other and you should too.

Here's what to do. Buy a pack of 5x8-inch file cards (they usually come 100 per pack, enough to start), a simple set of A to Z card indexes, and a metal file box to house them in. Complete a card for each and every piece you sell...full painting or simple sketch, large or small, high priced or low priced... every one! Let me tell you, I guarantee that you will refer to this file box time and time again because it has so much information on it. Let's review it space by space:

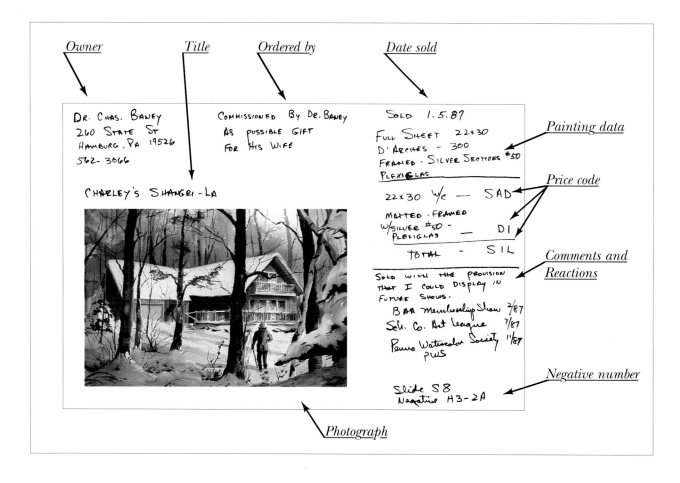

Owner   *Title*   *Ordered by*   *Date sold*

Dr. Chas. Baney
260 State St
Hamburg, Pa 19526
562-3066

Commissioned by Dr. Baney
as possible gift for his wife

Sold 1.5.87

Charley's Shangri-La

Painting data

Full Sheet   22x30
D'Arches - 300
Framed - Silver Sections #50
Plexiglas

Price code

22x30 w/c — SAD

Matted - Framed
w/silver #50 - — DI
Plexiglas

Total - SIL

Comments and Reactions

Sold with the provision that I could display in future shows.

BAA Membership Show 7/87
Sch. Co. Art League 7/87
Penna Watercolor Society 11/87
PWS

Negative number

Slide 58
Negative H3-2A

Photograph

Owner—List here the person who actually owns the painting. That person usually is the direct purchaser; however, there may be times when someone else may have purchased (or commissioned) the painting as a gift, so list here the ultimate owner. You'll need the owner's name in case a customer says, "I saw the painting you did for Pat Carpenter and want one like it."

Ordered by—This space is used to record special circumstances. If the painting was purchased or commissioned by someone as a gift to the owner, then record that person's name here. You may get repeat business from that person.

Date—You decide what dates you want to list here, dates that will serve your information needs. It could be the date commissioned, date delivered, or date you were paid—record any one or all three at your discretion.

Painting data—From the information recorded here I can tell what size the painting is, what paper and kind of mat I used, and how it was framed. This is important because sometimes a client will buy another watercolor and will want to pair it with a previous painting. They're sometimes hurt if you tell them you can't remember what you did for them before.

Price code—This is a holdover from my former marketing days. Once a painting has been sold, I am reluctant to place a figure out where one and all can see it. There are times when I may show someone else my art sold bin, so I code the sale price.

Your philosophy of pricing may change from time to time and when it does some of your paintings recorded in the file may show an embarrassingly low price or an opportunistic high price, and that really isn't anybody's business but yours. Also, your customers might not like if you let someone else know what they paid (especially in a town small enough that everyone knows each other).

You might feel that handling or deciphering a code is a nuisance but it really isn't; once you start using it with frequency, deciphering the figure is easy. I'm going to list a code you might use. It isn't what I use, but it is a suggestion. You can devise your own if you choose:

$$A\ R\ T\ S\ O\ L\ D\ B\ I\ N$$
$$1\ 2\ 3\ 4\ 5\ 6\ 7\ 8\ 9\ 0$$

Let's look at a sample. Your price code might look like this:

$$R\ A\ D$$
$$+\ O\ R$$
$$\text{TOTAL } R\ L\ I$$

That translates into:
$$\$217$$
$$+\ \$\ 52$$
$$\text{TOTAL } \$269$$

There now, that's not so tough, is it?

You can use any combination of catchy words when creating your own code as long as it is easy to remember. Be sure that none of the letters repeat and that the catchy word phrase is only ten letters long.

You can use this code as part of your selling information. I don't recommend haggling, dickering, or bargaining for a sales price. However, there may be a situation when an appropriate adjustment might be made, and I emphasize the word *adjustment* instead of *reduction*. You might put a selling price of $278 on your tag and in small letters code it to RAB ($218) as the lowest price you would consider selling it. (If you already have your bottom price firmly established in your mind, you'll be less likely to give in when a customer tries to push the price too low.)

Comments and reactions—Here is where you should record any unusual notes that need to be recalled, and of course reactions are always most welcome. You'll get those unsolicited favorable reactions, so by all means record them. There is no greater compliment than when the person on the street, unschooled in the 'isms of art, buys your painting because he or she likes it…and tells you so. By all means cherish those comments and record them to savor and enjoy when you struggle with a down period.

Negative number—I maintain a file of my photo negatives and slides and record the number on the reverse side of the photograph. There are times when you want to make several reprints and having this number makes it so much easier to locate the correct negative or slide. You may want reprints for a promotional folder, to show a client, to complete a scrapbook, or as a guide for another watercolor.

Title—I don't think it's necessary to assign titles to paintings, but if you do, this is a good place to put it.

Back of the card—If you need more room for any of the above information you can always use the reverse side. Or you can use the reverse side for more private or intimate notes because the casual reader usually doesn't flip the card.

Photograph—Last but not least—in fact one of the most important items for the card— is a photograph of the artwork itself. (I'll deal with taking the photograph in the next section.)

What if you don't have a photograph? Sometimes, when you sell the smaller pieces such as good sketches, you don't always have the time to photograph the artwork. At times like this you can still complete the card with a word description of the subject matter, enough so that you can recall the artwork.

This card layout is not etched in stone. This is the information that I place on my art sold card. It may serve as the stimulus for a design of your own.

Hauled Out for Repairs,
15x22 inches,
watercolor.

I recommend photographing every painting you do as soon as it's finished. You may not have time after it's been sold and could never get another chance. If I didn't have any paintings of nautical subjects on hand to show a customer interested in those subjects, I could use a slide of a painting like this one to show how I handle boats.

PHOTOGRAPHING YOUR ART

When I started painting in watercolors I never gave a second thought to taking photographs of my work in either print or slide form. As a result, early on I missed recording some of the pieces I sold. Then I started to enter juried exhibits, and they require that you submit slides of your entries. I had to start photographing my work and fast.

In addition to producing slides for juried exhibition entries, you'll want slides to use during presentations to clients and galleries. You will also want to produce slides to use in your illustrated presentations to civic groups about art in general and your art in particular (see Chapter 6). You will also want to produce good quality colored prints of your work for your own record in your art sold bin.

You will refer to this print time and time again so you might as well make it as professional as you can. *It is important!* You'll be surprised when you see a good photograph of your work. Your work will be seen in a new light (no pun intended). The even light will emphasize the painting's rich color and detail. Your eye will be concentrated on the subject matter and not be distracted by the environment of your painting area. This new and different vision will make the whole procedure worthwhile.

When I started photographing my paintings, I never thought about photographing indoors; I used to photograph outdoors on a sunny day on a rather hit-or-miss basis. It didn't take too long before I realized the importance of doing it indoors, in a controlled situation, and the re-

sults were dramatically improved and consistent. The task is really quite simple. Now don't throw up your hands in dismay, you can do it! You learned to paint, didn't you?

For those of you who do not photograph your artwork, or do no photographic work at all, I'll take you through the basic procedure. For more detailed information there are several guides and books on the subject, such as *Photographing Your Artwork*, by Russell Hart (North Light Books, listed in the Bibliography). This book as well as others can teach you how to do a professional job that will serve your needs.

Using the wrong film or lighting can result in an undesirable color cast, as shown by these two slides of the same painting. Since many jurors never see the actual painting, a poor slide can damage your chances of being accepted to a juried show.

If you still have doubts after reading up on the subject, I suggest you take your equipment list to a good reliable camera store and place yourself in the hands of knowledgeable sales personnel, who will gladly guide you through the whole process. You may be able to buy your equipment cheaper from the discount houses but all you'll get is equipment and no advice or help. At the camera shop you'll pay more, but you'll also have their personnel to guide you every step of the way. They will be available in the future to solve your problems as they arise and improve your results. You'll save money in the long run. Here is a list of what you'll need:

■ *Camera.* A 35mm single lens reflex (SLR) camera is a must. It need not be the expensive, top-of-the-line model with all the automatic features. A basic SLR camera with manual con-

Make sure your painting fills the frame when photographing your artwork. Unnecessary background like this distracts the jurors from what they should be looking at.

trols will do fine ($200 range).
■ *Lens.* The camera will usually be equipped with a 50mm lens. With this lens you can usually take your indoor shots and meet all your other general photography needs outdoors. I also use a lens that zooms from 80mm to 200mm in the studio ($175 range). When photographing several sizes of paintings it permits you to keep your tripod in one spot; you do not need to move it back and forth in order to properly fill the viewfinder with a larger or smaller painting. This is a great timesaver.
■ *A steady tripod.* Because some of your exposures may be from ½ second to ¹/₃₀ second in length, you cannot hand hold your camera without a wiggle. Your camera must not move even a minute amount; it must be steady. A tripod allows this.
■ *A cable release.* This too is necessary so you can trip the shutter without moving the camera. Your finger movement on the shutter release can jar the camera slightly, a problem at those slow speeds.
■ *Two clip-on dish reflectors.* These should be ten to twelve inches in diameter with 500 watt tungsten bulbs (3200K). Buy these bulbs in pairs and use them in pairs; if one burns out, replace the two. This will always assure you of even light temperatures.
■ *Two stands.* There are telescoping stands available on which you will clamp the above reflectors; if you are clever with your hands and some basic tools you can make vertical stands that will serve to support the clamp-on lamps. You could even clamp them on a chair back.
■ *Gray card.* This is held in front of your painting and the light meter on your camera measures the reflected light

from it so that the camera can be set at the proper lens opening and the proper shutter speed.
■ *Film for slides.* I like to use Kodak 160 Tungsten Ektachrome slide film and a setting of F11 at ¹/₃₀ and sometimes at ¹/₁₅, which produces the best results for me. This requires no filter because the film is balanced for the tungsten light supplied by your 500 watt (3200K) lamps.
■ *Film for prints.* I get good results with Kodacolor VRG (ISO 100). This film is color balanced for outdoor light so you must use an 80A color compensating filter when you photograph with the tungsten lights listed above.

The diagram on the next page illustrates the locations of lights and distances that will produce the best results.

Keep your room lights on (and your tungsten lights off) while setting up. Turn room lights off, and your tungsten lights on while getting a meter reading and exposing the film. You must not mix the two light sources.

Bracket your exposures. By that, I mean take three different exposures; one at the exposure indicated by the camera meter, one a half stop above and one a half stop below the meter setting. Also, take several shots of each painting. You will need duplicate slides from time to time. It will be easier and cheaper to take a half dozen exposures while you are photographing the painting than to send one slide out to a laboratory to make six duplicates, which won't have the same quality as the originals.

Record each shot in a notebook. When your slides and prints are returned they will be in the order in which you shot them. You can then mark them and compare them with the data in your notebook and determine which settings usually produce the best results.

When photographing your watercolors for publication in periodicals or books, it is helpful to include color bars in the slide, as shown at right. Most larger photographic stores stock them. These bars will help the editor determine which of several exposures is the correct one and allow the printer to check for accurate color during color separation. All this photography work sounds complicated and time consuming but it really isn't too difficult, and having good photographs of your paintings is worth the effort.

Print Shop,
Williamsburg, Virginia,
15 x 22 inches,
watercolor.

When photographing your watercolors for publication in periodicals or books, include color bars in the slide as I've done here so the color separator can tell when the color is correct.

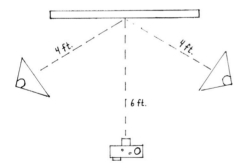

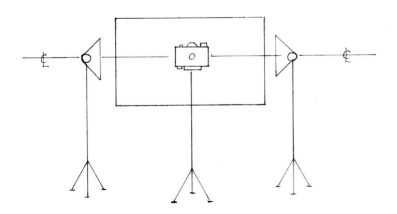

Here's how to set up your camera and lights to produce professional results when photographing your art. The camera is an SLR on a tripod and the lights are clamp-on dish reflectors with 500 watt tungsten bulbs on telescoping stands.

CHAPTER 9

L*et's talk about pricing*

■ "How do you price your paintings?" is one of the questions artists most frequently ask one another. I have a friend who is famous for his cliché which says, "Prices are like wages and rents…too much when you have to pay them, and not enough when you get them!" How true; there is no simple answer. There are no texts or manuals telling you "how to" or "what to" do about pricing because each person's situation is different—so much so that all I can do here is speak in generalities. But first you must ask some questions of yourself and seek the answers as objectively as you can.

What financial rewards are you expecting from your paintings? Enough for your entire livelihood? Half of your income? Twenty-five percent of your income? Just a few sales now and then? How much? This answer will be a factor to consider when you start a pricing policy.

The thrust of this book has been on helping you to succeed as an artist in your own hometown. Success doesn't always mean a lot of money, although that is part of it. Success is being able to put your paintings within the reach of everyone—by doing this you gain more than making a living. You gain the feeling that you are a part of a world that needs what you have to offer…you are sharing the ability you have with as many people as possible.

Are you objective enough to compare your work with similar paintings offered in your area at the open-air art fairs, at the mall sales, and at the galleries? *You must be!* Study and note the price ranges and then make a frank judgment—will your work support that price range? Higher? Lower? *Be honest!* Your prices must be commensurate with the level of your skills and with the prices accepted in your area or market.

Try to compare prices in areas similar to your own. If you live in a very small town that is not a city suburb, but is in a rather sparsely populated area of your state, you cannot compare prices with regions such as the resort area at the seashore. Check the galleries in the cities closest to you. These are professional business people and know what their potential customers are able and willing to pay. Use this as a starting place and adjust your prices for your own circumstances.

A work of art creates an emotional response for the viewer and there is no scientific method of determining how much emotion is worth in dollars and cents. However, there is one thing for certain…that painting that creates the emotional response is *worth the price that the viewer is willing to pay for it.* Now, whether you sell it for that mythical price, be it higher or lower than your expectations, is up to you.

Davidson Shop,
Williamsburg, Virginia,
15x22 inches,
watercolor.
The Cranford collection.

A painting of an out-of-town location, such as this scene in Williamsburg, Virginia, is hard to sell in Hamburg. I did this one for fun, but if I wanted to sell it I'd price it lower than paintings of local scenes. This is an earlier watercolor, and I can see now that it would be much more interesting if I had added several figures.

PRESTIGE OR SALES?

It took me a long time to accept that statement...a painting is worth what the viewer is willing to pay for it! But it's true, and you too must be willing to accept that statement if you want to sell your paintings. It is the painting's value to the customer that sets the price, not its value to you.

If you are a working painter it will not take too long for that unsold pile of paintings to grow. You keep painting but the selling is slow. In that case either the quality of your work or the price isn't right. If the quality is comparable to what is offered in your area, then it must be the price and no matter how painful, you may have to adjust your prices. Consider this hypothetical question—would I rather have this painting hanging for sale at $500 for two years (or four) or would I rather sell it for $100 *now!* By selling a few paintings at $100, I can obtain the funds that will permit me to continue to grow and paint more and more, funds to be used to enhance my library, attend that special workshop, and more.

Only you can make that decision. Remember that no price level is forever. As your skills, ability, and recognition increase then the prices will increase. *Recognition!* Isn't that what we are striving for? When you are totally involved in painting the style and subject matter that interests the people in your market area, when you are enthusiastic about it and creative too, people will become interested. They will want your work because *you did it.* You will have created an emotional response for them...and that is what art is all about.

But, you say, selling your paintings at prices that are very low is "like giving your work away, selling them too cheap." Not at all. What I am suggesting is that you price your paintings at a practical level, *low enough so they will sell.* It is useless and unproductive to try to sell them at those "sophisticated and arty" prices that you often see at exhibitions. I'm sure you have been to art association exhibits and other non-juried shows where the prices may vary from $70 to $700 to $7,000.

Starting artists have a tendency to overprice their work thinking that prices very, very high will impress prospective buyers as well as their peers. Permit me to make this facetious comment—when I paint like Andrew Wyeth and when I have achieved the same acceptance and recognition as Andrew Wyeth, then I too can expect that my paintings will bring Andrew Wyeth prices. There are very few clients who judge the merits of a painting by its price tag...it must be good because its price is so high...and you really don't want to sell to that person anyway.

If you start with realistic prices and raise them as your skills and reputation grow, customers who bought early pieces will feel they made a good investment, increasing their satisfaction with their purchase—and there's no better publicity than a satisfied customer.

My Nephew Mike Lives Here, 15x22 inches, watercolor.

This client has a number of my paintings in her collection and I took that fact into consideration when I established the price for this commission.

BE UNIFORM

When you do establish a pricing pattern, be consistent and uniform. The public and your clients lose confidence and interest in you when they see prices that vacillate from high to low and reverse. In smaller areas the clients do get to see each other; in fact, many of your sales will be made because a satisfied customer tells a neighbor or a friend and in cases such as this they will compare prices.

Another point you must remember is that a satisfied client is always a potential repeat buyer of a second, third (or more) painting. If that first painting had an unrealistic price tag the buyer may not be interested in another; customers do like to hang paintings in pairs or groups. In fact, you must be consistent not only in your pricing but in all other aspects of your dealings with clients. They do compare notes.

BE A LITTLE DIFFERENT, TOO

Have you noticed in prior paragraphs I discussed prices such as $50, $500, $700, and $7,000? I don't price that way because the figures are all rounded and they sound so whimsical…they sound like amounts that were just pulled out of the air. Conversely, I don't recommend typical retail store pricing such as $99.50 instead of $100 or $198 instead of $200. I do suggest a figure that sounds as though some cost analysis was used in establishing the price. Some examples might be these: Instead of $400, try $385 or $410; not $200, but $190 or $215; even $100 doesn't work too well, try $125 or $90.

My Pennsylvania Roots, 15x22 inches, watercolor. The George collection.

Here again, a watercolor reminds someone of their roots. This was also purchased by a repeat customer. Many of my customers come back to me for other paintings after they've purchased the first one and I always keep that in mind when fixing the price.

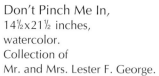

Don't Pinch Me In,
14½x21½ inches,
watercolor.
Collection of
Mr. and Mrs. Lester F. George.

People often ask, "How long does it take to paint something like that?" They don't realize how much work is involved before you begin to put pigment to paper. It took a long time and a lot of work before I started to paint this one. This house, pinched and crowded by its neighbors, faces west. I passed it one day and noticed that when the sun goes down during the winter some interesting shadows are thrown on the house. I made a mental note to come back the next day with my camera, since this street is too busy to make a sketch on the spot. I returned every day for two weeks, but the sun never did. I finally decided to go ahead without it. I developed a value sketch from the photograph and then did a color sketch to make sure I could re-create the colors and shadows accurately. You and I both know some paintings take this much work, but it is up to us to patiently explain the process to the customer so they understand just what they're buying.

PRICE RANGE FOR COMMISSIONS

When I am asked how much I charge to do a painting, let's say a house portrait, I rarely quote a *firm price*. I very carefully explain that I will not know final costs until the painting is finished because the price is dependent upon these factors:

■ How much preliminary work I may have to do—which means study, research, and, most important, preliminary sketches.

■ The amount of time to execute the painting.

■ The amount of material.

■ The quality of the final result.

And then I explain that while I don't quote a firm price I do quote a price range based upon previous commissions, minimum to maximum. For example, if I know from past experience that a painting such as they want will sell (matted only, unframed) for $240 I will quote from $210 to $270 and the client will accept that. I've never had one turn me down.

BARGAIN OR BARTER?

This is a very sensitive area and only you can make the decision. The terms are different. In our area people don't bargain—we call it "dickering"—same thing. I don't do it, but that doesn't mean that you cannot or shall not. Some artists swear by it and at open exhibitions encourage it as well as accept it, and they seem to enjoy it. (Here is another way that the pricing code we discussed on page 99 will be helpful—by allowing you to put your "lowest price" in code on your price tag, in addition to your selling price.)

As I stated before, I do not bargain, haggle, or dicker over prices with a prospective customer. Having researched my market as I explained earlier, I establish what I think is a fair and firm price and that is the price that I put on my price sticker for that painting.

There are some artists who try to elicit a reaction from a customer before naming a price; this way they may be able to add an extra $25 or $50 or $75 to their original price if the customer seems especially taken with a piece. I don't do this because I feel my price is a fair one, established after considerable market study and analysis. It's not fair to the customer either, and I suggest to you to be careful with this practice because customers do on occasion get together and compare notes.

I price my commercial work in the same manner. I don't treat those clients any different than my private clientele. Don't charge a bank an extra hidden amount just because it is a bank and has the ability to pay more.

Bartering is something else again. I have exchanged paintings for professional services rendered as well as for merchandise. On one occasion I was in need of some accounting and tax work and the small accounting firm that did the work was very much interested in trading services; in fact, they suggested the mutual exchange. Another time I consulted a financial consultant for some advice that required extensive research in addition to her expertise. Here again the client suggested the barter when she learned about my watercolors.

Another opportunity for barter arose quite by accident one time when I was purchasing a portable electric typewriter. The dealer quoted the price and quite casually I remarked, "Gee, that's just about what some of my watercolors sell for. I'll have to get busy and create another one to pay for this. You don't happen to need an anniversary present for your wife, or a wedding present for someone?" I struck a nerve...yes, he did need an anniversary present and he wanted to know how we could arrange an exchange. I invited him to my living room gallery. He came sooner than I expected (during his lunch break) and with his wife. The anniversary present wasn't for his wife but for his wife's parents' golden wedding anniversary. They reviewed the paintings, made a selection, and we made a mutually satisfactory trade. They were delighted! They had solved the age-old problem of "what do you buy for someone who has everything?" I was delighted because it solved a temporary cash flow problem I had.

Small businesses are often more receptive to barter because they encounter more cash flow problems than "the big boys" do. I've also found that it is easier to barter for services than for products. Remember, you still have tax responsibilities even during transactions such as these. You must establish a fair value for both parts of the barter. You must report your barter receipt as income and you must treat your barter expenditure the same as if you had spent cash. Your tax preparer can help you with this.

"HOW LONG DOES IT TAKE?"

How often have you been asked, "How long does it take you to paint a picture like that?" Plenty, I'm sure. When I'm asked that, I reply, "Ten hours...and twenty years." You know and I know what I mean by that, but be sure to patiently explain to the observer what an answer like that means. Remember, the observer's intention was utter friendliness—the person is trying to find some common ground, and is reaching out in an effort to express admiration for your work. No matter how tiring the repeated question might be, don't react curtly. The average viewer has little contact with artists and has very little understanding of what you are trying to do, but they are curious and they are interested.

If you give an answer like mine, patiently tell them that "ten hours...and twenty years" means that while the actual execution of the painting took about ten hours, you have been painting and studying a long time (maybe even longer than twenty years) to develop the skills necessary to transfer your thoughts onto paper and create an image that is exciting and a joy to behold. That image may be a special mood, a colorful abstract, a factual representation, or a delicate and rare thing of beauty. All twenty years of painting and learning went into the piece they're looking at.

Be sure to explain how long you spend *thinking* about the idea or concept, make plain the need for the many *preliminary sketches* you might do, the research that is often called for, and be sure to explain that it often takes more time to *draw the subject* than it does to paint it (particularly the "village scene"). If you just answer the question directly and say you painted the piece in X number of hours, your customers may underestimate the effort that went into it and could think you're overcharging them. This discussion usually uncovers the latent interest they have in art and makes them more aware of the joy that can be theirs when they purchase a painting, and especially a painting created by you.

Law Office, 64 N. Fourth St., 11x7½ inches, watercolor.

I've never painted a door as a commissioned effort; I do them because I like to. But the door paintings sell well, and because they cost less than a full house portrait they sometimes open doors to potential customers who might not otherwise consider buying a painting. Once they discover the joy of owning an original painting, they often commission others!

GIVING PAINTINGS AWAY

There are times when it may be to your advantage to give a painting away as a door prize or maybe a prize for a club lottery, bingo, or other money-raising event. Such a donation can help out a cause you believe in as well as spread your reputation, but be very careful and analytical when these requests are made because you don't want to start a custom. If you give a painting as a prize to one organization it may be difficult for you to tactfully turn down a request from another one...they all are worthy, they all need help.

Instead, it may be possible or feasible to have someone sponsor that donation to the organization's fund-raising drive. The sponsor pays for the painting and donates it to the organization—the sponsor has the pleasure of knowing that his or her donation helped raise additional funds for the organization and your painting serves as a unique attention-getter for the fund-raising drive.

Giving gifts to some of your friends and not to others can also create some delicate situations. An iron-clad policy on giving away paintings is difficult to adhere to because you may have to bend it sometime, but if you do have to deviate from the norm do it as tactfully as you can.

Keep in mind that your paintings have value, both financial and aesthetic. If you give them away too often, you may come to undervalue your own work. Don't let that happen. If you don't appreciate the paintings' value, how can the public?

CONCLUSION

I know of no better way to end this chapter than to emphasize that you must focus on two important steps to selling your work.

First, you must display your work again and again where as many people as possible can view it...and by people I don't mean other artists. I mean people in general—all kinds of people!

Second, your work must be priced so that these same people (all kinds of people) can buy the one they want.

CHAPTER 10

A walk around town

■ What follows is a collection of paintings based on scenes in and around Hamburg, Pennsylvania. But before I tell you what this section will be, let me tell you what it won't be.

This section will *not* be a gallery of exceptional watercolors painted by other artists that are meant to demonstrate all the elements that good paintings should have. All the paintings in this section are my own, and they're certainly not meant to serve as models for how you should paint.

This section will *not* be a portfolio of my watercolors with captions to slyly show you how accomplished I am—I will be the first to admit I am still in the learning process. That doesn't bother me because all the accomplished artists I know and have studied with will tell you they are still in (and will always be in) the learning process. It never ends.

This section *will* be devoted to showing you more watercolors and sketches of subject areas in and around my hometown. These are in addition to those on previous pages, although a few are repeated in order to further emphasize a point.

It is my hope that by looking at what I've chosen to paint in and around Hamburg, including some photographs of the real scenes and some of the preliminary sketches I made, you can get ideas for subjects you can paint in your own town.

I'll show you scenes I overlooked for years because of my own "eyeball rut" and scenes that aren't pretty in the usual sense but which have produced interesting paintings. I'll include paintings done at different stages of my own growth and some that turned out better than others, so

you'll see that you don't have to be at the point of perfection before you begin selling your work.

I'm not trying to suggest that you should mimic Stew Biehl (or John Wenger or Zoltan Szabo or anyone else). Many of the ideas I've used can be adapted to whatever your style or subject or medium. They can get your inspiration wheels turning. For instance, you may look at my painting of Hamburg's five-and-dime and decide to paint a still life of items from the shelves of such a store in your town. You may see the painting of our weekly newspaper's former offices and get the idea for a montage that uses bits of your local paper. That's terrific! Work on your own ideas and let your creativity flow.

So let's take a walk around town!

Architectural Potpourri,
15x22 inches,
watercolor.
Courtesy of Mr. and Mrs. Mark Leiby.

Every time I take my car out of the garage and turn the corner I must stop at this signal light. I must have seen this view at least 5,000 times and seen nothing. But one day it hit me...I was fascinated by the difference in roof lines and changed the color of one roof to emphasize the effect.

Shomo's Alley,
pencil sketch.

Shomo's Alley,
27 x 21 inches,
ink line and watercolor.
Collection of the artist.

Every little town has its share of attractive houses, colorful flower beds, covered bridges, or pastoral landscapes. Every little town also has its sections that are a bit scruffy, like our Shomo's Alley. Don't overlook the scruffy areas when looking for subject matter. I made the pencil sketch of this alley about twenty-five years ago. Things have changed since then, giving it even more character, so I painted it again in ink line and watercolor. This spot struck a responsive chord with several other local people and I've sold several variations on this scene.

American Shoe Repair Shop,
15x22 inches,
watercolor.
Collection of
Mr. and Mrs. J. Carl Borelli.

This appears to be a painting of these retail establishments. It isn't—it is a painting of emotion, of the heart. Most juried shows would pass it over, but I couldn't care less. It is one of the most "successful" I've ever done. The white building was the shop and residence of Mr. and Mrs. Carl Borelli. He was an immigrant bootmaker and later shoe repairman. The Borelli family touched the lives of everyone in our town: Jenny was a soprano extraordinaire; Joe a musician, teacher, and conductor par excellence; and Madeline a fifth-grade teacher who taught me, my children, and most of the people in Hamburg. Do you have stories such as this in your village? Of course you do.

Wagner's Department Store,
1907-1970,
14½x21½ inches,
watercolor.
Collection of Arabel Wagner Diament.

Nostalgia, roots, sentimentality—all are good reasons why people buy paintings. This painting was commissioned by the founder's granddaughter and shows the store the way it looked shortly before it went out of business in 1970.

This color sketch shows another downtown business scene that's just waiting to be painted, the Hamilton Bank. Paintings of commercial buildings are almost as popular as those of private homes.

Dusk Settles on St. John's,
14¼ x 21¼ inches,
watercolor.
Collection of the artist.

Sometimes a special mood changes an ordinary scene or angle into a real possibility. I was returning to town one day via Pine Street and the beautiful sky speeded me up…yes, speeded me up so I could rush home, grab my camera, return, and make a photo. I returned later to take another photograph in snow because that's how I wanted to paint the scene. As you can see from the photographs, I moved a small stream in the foreground and made it larger to get the reflection I wanted. I also brought the building on the left edge into the scene to improve the composition.

Berne United Methodist Church,
15x22 inches,
watercolor.

This is a small church about two miles west of Hamburg in a lovely rural setting. I wanted to preserve that rural feeling so I gave it a fall mood. The church council purchased this painting.

First United Church of Christ,
22x15 inches,
watercolor.

Churches are a familiar subject in every locale and they are dearly loved by their parishioners. For the most part you have to be true to the scene when painting churches, but you can add colorful skies, put in a few figures for interest, or add or delete a few trees to improve color or framing.

Salem Evangelical Congregational
Church,
15x22 inches,
watercolor.

Jay Jerome Miller House,
11x15 inches,
watercolor.

In towns like Hamburg, houses were built side by side so that none of the important agricultural land was wasted. As a result, most of my house portraits include bits of the neighboring buildings—it wouldn't be realistic to paint the houses in isolation.

Four Hundred and Thirty North Fifth Street,
15x22 inches,
watercolor.
Courtesy of
Mr. and Mrs. Leroy C. Dietrich.

Even if you don't live in a village that is steeped in historical housing, you still can find many settings that are interesting and that will touch someone in a personal way, and that person will be in your own backyard.

Drive-In Window,
22x30 inches,
watercolor.
Collection of
Hamburg Savings and Trust Co.

The Hamburg Savings and Trust Co. wanted me to paint every location, including this modern drive-in branch. Subjects like this can be every bit as challenging and rewarding as those you choose to paint if you don't let the opinions of the so-called art critics get in your way.

Bootmaker's Shop, Williamsburg, Virginia,
11x14 inches,
graphite pencil.

When you walk the streets of Williamsburg, Virginia, the painting possibilities are endless. Every building is surrounded by an aura of history, trees are expertly trimmed, and grounds are beautifully manicured. But you can find settings of similar beauty in your home-town—try to look at your own town as if you were a tourist and see what you find. The Miller-Bausher House is every bit as lovely as Williamsburg's boot-maker's shop, isn't it?

Miller-Bausher House,
15x22 inches,
watercolor.
Courtesy of Michael Fryer.

This sketch is put in here to remind you to be ever cognizant of details as you look around town. A subject like this can be rendered well in ink line and watercolor wash.

Pig Iron, Sand and Coke,
14½x21½,
watercolor.
Collection of Mr. and Mrs. Carl A. Francis.

Industries present opportunities for more than one painting. This one has all the elements needed to make several watercolors. But you ask, "Who buys paintings such as this?" All the employees of the foundry are potential customers. In this instance, the plant manager's wife purchased the painting as a birthday present.

This is a color sketch of the back lot of a neighboring industry. I plan to paint a series of at least six watercolors of this industry.

Bank and Annex, Circa 1912,
22x30 inches,
watercolor.
Collection of Hamburg Savings and
Trust Co.

Be aware of the changes in your community because they present many opportunities for watercolors. This painting was developed from the few old photographs that exist; compare it to the current scene as shown in the photograph.

Here is a classic case of the village scene that is constantly undergoing change. The corner building in "Wagners and Wengerts Corner" (below) was built as a meat market and throughout the years housed a photographic studio, insurance office, barbershop, and a long list of delicatessens, luncheonettes, and sweet shops. The house next to it has served as residence and office space for several doctors and lawyers. Dr. Moll, a local dentist, needed permanent office quarters so he bought the corner building and replaced it with the colonial building shown in "Dr. Moll's Corner" (left). I painted both the before and after scenes.

Dr. Moll's Corner,
15x22 inches,
watercolor.

Wagners and Wengerts Corner,
14½x21½ inches,
watercolor.

Reflections on Something Old,
21x27 inches,
watercolor.
Private collection.

Landmarks such as this building, which has been in continuous use for a century or more, make excellent subject matter. This one now houses an antiques shop, appropriately enough.

Publishing Since 1875 in
Lemon Alley,
21x27 inches,
watercolor.
Private collection.

"The Hamburg Item" is our weekly newspaper and has been published since 1875, starting here on the corner of Lemon Alley.

Reading Railroad Passenger and
Freight Station,
15x22 inches,
ink line and watercolor wash.
Private collection.

The number of railroad buffs is almost limitless, as are the sales possibilities for paintings like this one. This station has been converted to private use, but this is what it looked like when activity was at its peak.

Jake's Barber Shop,
11 x 7½ inches,
watercolor.

Barbershops are places that hold fond memories for many people, and they offer lots of painting possibilities, whether it's a portrait of the town's long-time barber, a sketch of a youngster getting that first haircut, a still life of scissors and razors, or something along the lines of what I've done.

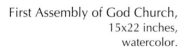

First Assembly of God Church,
15x22 inches,
watercolor.

Windsor Press,
15x22 inches,
watercolor.
Courtesy of William Mitten.

Institutions are constantly adding to their structures or remodeling and this provides a good opportunity to suggest a painting. The painting of the First Assembly of God Church was done just after the church added a new wing. The Windsor Press building is on a busy corner and seems to be changing constantly, so I painted it after the most recent renovation.

Costigan's Wagon Shed,
22x30 inches,
watercolor.

These two treatments of the same wagon shed show how much variety can be found on just one farm. While the angle changed only slightly, the difference in mediums makes a big difference in the mood conveyed.

Costigan's Wagon Shed,
11x14 inches,
graphite pencil.

Jake's Beehives,
15x22 inches,
watercolor.

When you think of beehives you probably imagine them in a fruit orchard where they are needed for pollination. These hives were in an alfalfa field in this protective swale and the bees were as busy as can be...I maintained a respectful distance.

New Red Door, Fuller's Barn #2,
22x30 inches,
watercolor.

I've painted many scenes on this farm, including this view of the barn with a newly painted red door. Ageless scenes such as this always are well received—don't refuse to paint them simply because they've been done before.

Dreibelbis Bridge,
11x14 inches,
graphite pencil.

*Seaside painters have their No. 1
motif—the beach at Rockpoint,
Massachusetts. Countryside
landscape painters have a No. 1
motif, too—the covered bridge. The
avant-garde painters wrinkle their
noses and show jurors pass them
by, but what's important is that
the public likes paintings like
these. There are times when you
must determine which you want,
acclaim or sales.*

Fishin' Hole,
11x15 inches,
watercolor.

These two color sketches of the same barn show the importance of making such sketches. Here I'm experimenting with color and key to see what works best for this setting.

Spring House,
22x30 inches,
watercolor.

Sometimes an overall scene attracts my eye, but occasionally a tighter view such as this corner of a spring house yields a good painting. I find paintings like this one somewhat harder to sell because they aren't a scene that's easily recognized as local.

Rural Electric,
21½x29½ inches,
watercolor.

Your watercolor sheet doesn't have to be covered by pretty pastel-colored washes to be interesting. This scene features one of the transmission lines that feed electric power to our area. One viewer summed it up perfectly when she said, "I never realized a painting of wires could be so interesting."

Passing Storm,
11x15 inches,
watercolor.

Sometimes what happens in the sky is as interesting, sometimes more so, as what you see on the ground. I tried to capture that here.

BIBLIOGRAPHY

These books are not arranged in alphabetical order. They are arranged in the order that I suggest they be added to your library.

■ *Watercolor: You Can Do It!*
Couch, Tony. Cincinnati, Ohio: North Light Books, 1987.

If a watercolor beginner were to ask me, "Which book should I buy first?" I would recommend this as No. 1. Maybe I'm prejudiced because I've attended four of Tony's workshops. I like the free, easy drawing style; the juicy watercolor appearance; and the pleasing end results of Tony's methods.

■ *Watercolor Techniques Workbooks.*
Couch, Tony. Cincinnati, Ohio: North Light Books, 1989.

These two workbooks actually contain ten complete projects with pre-drawn sketches where you paint right alongside the author, step by step. This is a very innovative approach and a very helpful learning tool. I wish it had been available years ago when I started.

■ *Ways With Watercolors.*
Kautzky, Ted. New York: Reinhold Publishing Corp., 1949; second printing, May 1953.

I had been exposed to other watercolor books in the fifties, but when I bought this book I jumped ten feet high. I loved his sketches, paintings, and his style. They jumped out of the pages and said, paint...*paint* ...PAINT! I was especially impressed by the value studies

on page 15, tips on painting buildings. His method of teaching also helped me— using two colors, three colors, and finally four colors.

■ *Painting Trees and Landscapes in Watercolor*
Kautzky, Ted. New York: Reinhold Publishing Corp., 1952; sixth printing, 1960.

This book is a natural follow-up to *Ways with Watercolor.* The material on value arrangement on page 8 alone is worth the price of the book. This tells it all. The book has many of its chapters devoted to various kinds of trees and once again he includes a section devoted to practice subjects. This procedure is frowned upon by many watercolorists/authors but I like it. As a beginning watercolorist your sketches or drawings need just as much help as your watercolors do. When you are learning to design, draw, and paint all at one time, the results can be pretty dreary. These pre-drawn subjects help to bridge the gap.

■ *Kautzky: Master of Pencil and Watercolor.*
Kinghan, Charles R. Ted. New York: Reinhold Publishing Corp., 1959.

I fell in love with watercolor when I was exposed to books by and about Ted Kautzky. This book illustrates many of his value pencil sketches done in the broadside fashion. It also contains many architectural renderings, of the type that are of particular help to me. There are enough watercolors sprinkled throughout it to make me want to see more, so I sought out all the Kautzky books I could find.

■ *Landscape Painting in Watercolor.*
Szabo, Zoltan. New York: Watson-Guptill, 1971.

■ *Zoltan Szabo Paints Landscapes.*
Szabo, Zoltan. New York: Watson-Guptill, 1977.

■ *Zoltan Szabo: Artist at Work.*
Szabo, Zoltan. New York: Watson-Guptill, 1979.

I list only three of Zoltan Szabo's books here but I have five of them in my library and all of them will contribute greatly to your growth as an artist. I have been fortunate enough to attend two of his excellent workshops and have come to know him as a friend. I last saw him in 1985; we were having lunch in Union Deposit, Pennsylvania, on the last day of his workshop. His parting comment was "Stew, you'll make it, don't get discouraged. You have all the tools and skills but you lack one thing now—WORK! Go home now and really start to paint and all the pieces will start to fall into place." I was ever so appreciative of his comments even though he probably tells that to all of his students. I didn't care if he'd said it a thousand times before...it motivated me and I will always be grateful.

■ *Watercolor Painting Techniques*
Lewis, David. New York: Watson-Guptill, 1983.

This book is really a miniature art school with seven teachers presenting excerpts from their books: John Blockley, *Country Landscapes in Watercolor;* Richard Bolton, *Painting Weathered Textures in Watercolors;* Charles Reid, *Portrait Painting in Watercolor* and *Figure Painting in*

Watercolor; E. John Robinson, *How to Paint Seascapes in Watercolor;* Christopher Schink, *Mastering Color and Design in Watercolor;* Georg Shook, *Sharp Focus Watercolor Painting;* and Zoltan Szabo, *Zoltan Szabo Paints Landscapes.*

■ *Watercolor Painting Step by Step*
Guptill, Arthur L. New York: Watson-Guptill, 1957.

This is a book that is short on illustrations and reproductions but long on text. I've had it in my library for many years. I bought it in 1960 and was disappointed at the time because it had so much text to read. But (and this is a big *but*) after I started reading and studying other books, I found myself returning to this volume more frequently. What he had to say thirty years ago is still relevant. I wouldn't give it up.

■ *Watercolor Lessons From Eliot O'Hara*
Schmalz, Carl. New York: Watson-Guptill, 1974.

Zoltan Szabo recommended this book to me because he felt it would be helpful for me to be exposed to Eliot O'Hara. All of his books are out of print so I went through a long search before I found this one. However, the result was well worthwhile for this book contains thirty-two lessons and watercolor reproductions. The lessons are simple, as are the watercolors; they are pure and free and yet they tell a complete story.

■ *Capturing Mood in Watercolor*
Austin, Phil. Cincinnati, Ohio: North Light Books, 1988.

Several things made this book so necessary for my library.

First his seven-color palette is most challenging and I return to this chapter frequently. This limited palette also explains why his colors are so fresh and appealing. Second, Phil Austin has the ability to take the mundane, or ordinary and commonplace landscape scenes and arrange them by design, color, and mood into lively pieces of art. These field and farm scenes are in Wisconsin but could be in Pennsylvania, Georgia, or any other state. I often review the book to get the creative juices flowing.

■ *Make Your Watercolors Sing*
Hutchings, LaVere. Cincinnati, Ohio: North Light Books, 1986.

I bought this book in 1986 and its value is twofold. It is a great book for the intermediate painter (and above) for two reasons. First, it has a lot of new color information, and second, his style helps to loosen up your paintings. As you continue to work alone you have a tendency to tighten up and this book reminds one to loosen up a bit; omit those details that you feel are so necessary. I especially love his comments on page 40 about a clean palette and why it is so important. I read it again from time to time.

■ *The Sketch*
Oliver, Robert S. New York: Van Nostrand Reinhold Co., 1979.

■ *The Sketch in Color*
Oliver, Robert S. New York: Van Nostrand Reinhold Co., 1983.

These two gems are a must for every watercolorist. Robert Oliver knows how to sketch in the simplest of forms and cuts

through and ignores all the unnecessary details that usually foul up a watercolor or painting.

■ *Putting People in Your Paintings*
Draper, Everett J. Cincinnati, Ohio: North Light Books, 1985.

■ *People Painting Scrapbook*
Draper, Everett J. Cincinnati, Ohio: North Light Books, 1988.

Some time ago I decided that I would insert life of some form in my paintings, some birds, maybe an animal, such as a dog or cat, but most often some people. These books will tell you how to do that and will start your creative efforts moving in that direction.

■ *John Blockley: Watercolor Interpretations*
Blockley, John. London: William Collins Sons & Co., 1987; Cincinnati: North Light Publishing, 1987.

This book needs to be in everybody's library and in a handy spot too. The style is loose, colorful, juicy, and free, and every now and then all painters must transfuse this into their work to eliminate the stiffness. Too often one slips into an artistic rut. This book will help to eliminate it.

I consider the following books to be inspirational books; these are the books that you can curl up with in a soft chair on a night when there isn't anything worthwhile on the telly, or maybe you just don't care to start another novel or whodunit. These books get the urges and creative juices flowing.

■ *Ranulph Bye's Bucks County*
Bye, Ranulph. Washington Crossing, Pennsylvania: Bargeron Publishing Inc., 1989.

■ *The Vanishing Depot*
Bye, Ranulph. Wayne, Pennsylvania: Haverford House, 1973.

■ *Victorian Sketchbook*
Bye, Ranulph. Wayne, Pennsylvania: Haverford House, 1980.

I have listed the books above in their order of interest and importance. These books are not art instruction books but are extremely helpful to some interested in painting the village scene. The first volume contains two hundred excellent watercolors of landmarks and village scenes in Bucks County. The second is a compilation of first-rate paintings of specific depots that are vanishing from the railroad scene. Many of the locations are known to me personally. The third is virtually the same thing but devoted to Victorian mansions, outbuildings, etc., throughout the Northeast. A study of this collection of skillfully rendered watercolors is certain to improve your own work.

■ *Watercolor*
Pike, John. New York: Watson-Guptill, 1966.

Every personal library should have the John Pike books in it. I could not afford any of his originals but by purchasing his two books I have a large collection of prints to enjoy over and over again. My one regret is that my interest in watercolor came too late, so that John Pike had passed away before I was able to attend one of his workshops. He tells you that he is a water, snow, and fog man and he paints them perfectly. When you look at his forest scenes you feel you can just walk right into the foreground and on through that hazy forest background. His diagram and watercolor on pages 132 and 133 teaches you how to acheive those same realistic results.

■ *John Pike Paints Watercolors*
Pike, John. New York: Watson-Guptill, 1978.

The comments above apply to this book too. However, since I missed his workshops, I do appreciate the introduction in this book, as well as the interview section, the portfolio of sketches on pages 33 through 44, and last but not least the gallery starting on page 120. I often get out my Pike books and "look at the pictures."

■ *Watercolorists at Work*
Meyer, Susan E. and Kent, Norman. New York: Watson-Guptill, 1972.

■ *40 Watercolorists and How They Work*
Meyer, Susan E. New York: Watson-Guptill, 1976.

■ *100 Watercolor Techniques*
Kent, Norman. New York: Watson-Guptill, 1968.

Watercolorists love to look at, review, and critique one another's work. You can do just that with these three books. These three books contain samples of work by 165 artists—a veritable museum of watercolors to be enjoyed again and again!

■ *Eighty: An American Souvenir*
Sloane, Eric. New York: Dodd, Mead, & Company, 1985.

I wish I had been able to meet Eric Sloane before he passed away because I admire his philosophy of art as well as his art. The book is liberally sprinkled with both.

■ *Living by Your Brush Alone.*
Piersol, Edna Wagner. Cincinnati, Ohio: North Light Books, 1989.

This book should be in your personal library. It will help you to decide whether you can or whether you even want to make painting a successful full-time career.

■ *Photographing Your Artwork*
Hart, Russell. Cincinnati, Ohio: North Light Books, 1987.

If you are going to become serious about your art, then you must become serious about photographing your art—for entering shows, keeping records, and many other purposes. This book is an easily understood text that shows how to get professional results.

RESOURCES

The artists whose works are reproduced in this book have been of great help and inspiration to me. If you want to get more information about their books, videos, and workshops I mentioned, here's how:

Ranulph Bye

Inquiries about his workshops and three books should be directed to: Ranulph Bye, P.O. Box 362, Mechanicsville, PA, 18934.

Tony Couch

Direct inquiries about workshops, books, and videotapes to:
5480 Musket Lane, Stone Mountain, GA, 30087.

Ginger Dancull Gouger

Inquiries about watercolors and stitcheries should be made to: Ginger & Spice, Box 303, Reading, PA, 19607.

Lynda K. Potter

Inquiries about Lynda's talents should be addressed to: Lynda K. Potter, 46 Fairway Drive, Rosehill Plantation, Bluffton, SC, 29910.

Zoltan Szabo

All inquiries about Zoltan Szabo's five books, workshops, and videos should be sent to: Willa McNeill, 5014 Coronado Drive, Charlotte, NC, 28212.

Frederick William Wetzel

Fred can be reached by contacting: Bernard Zang, Coordinator and Agent, R.D. #1, Box 39, Kempton, PA, 19529, (215)756-4325.

PERMISSIONS

Pages 29, 78:
Big Sister, Big Bite, and *In for Repairs*, by Tony Couch. Used by permission of the artist.

Pages 34, 88:
Unionville, Chester County; Horst's Mill; and *Old Courthouse, Newcastle, Delaware* by John Wenger. Used by permission of the artist.

Pages 42, 47:
Carversville, Solebury Township, Pennsylvania; New Hope Station, Pennsylvania; and *Bucks County Playhouse, New Hope*, by Ranulph Bye. Used by permission of the artist.

Page 50:
Winter Stroll, by Zoltan Szabo. Used by permission of the artist.

Page 60:
Blue Bird, by Mary C. Schappell. Used by permission of the artist.

Page 69:
Festiva Maxima and *Self Portrait*, by Lynda Potter. Used by permission of the artist.

Page 70:
Rough-Legged Hawk, by Frederick William Wetzel. Used by permission of the artist.

Page 73:
Broken Lanterns and *Autumn Lanterns*, by Regina Dancull Gouger. Used by permission of the artist.

Page 81:
Hotel Strater, Durango, Colorado and *Narrow Gauge*, by Russell Steel. Used by permission of the artist.

Page 82:
Approaching Storm at Sutliff's, by Mary Keiser. Used by permission of the artist.

INDEX

Other Art Books from North Light

Graphics/Business of Art

Airbrush Artist's Library (6 in series) $12.95 (cloth)
Airbrush Techniques Workbooks (8 in series) $9.95 each
Airbrushing the Human Form, by Andy Charlesworth $19.95 (cloth)
The Art & Craft of Greeting Cards, by Susan Evarts $15.95 (paper)
The Artist's Friendly Legal Guide, by Conner, Karlen, Perwin, & Spatt $15.95 (paper)
Artist's Market: Where & How to Sell Your Graphic Art (Annual Directory) $19.95 (cloth)
Basic Graphic Design & Paste-Up, by Jack Warren $13.95 (paper)
Color Harmony: A Guide to Creative Color Combinations, by Hideaki Chijiiwa $15.95 (paper)
Complete Airbrush & Photoretouching Manual, by Peter Owen & John Sutcliffe $24.95 (cloth)
The Complete Guide to Greeting Card Design & Illustration, by Eva Szela $27.95 (cloth)
Creating Dynamic Roughs, by Alan Swann $27.95 (cloth)
Creative Ad Design & Illustration, by Dick Ward $32.95 (cloth)
Creative Director's Sourcebook, by Nick Souter and Stuart Neuman $89.00 (cloth)
Creative Typography, by Marion March $27.95 (cloth)
Design Rendering Techniques, by Dick Powell $29.95 (cloth)
Dynamic Airbrush, by David Miller & James Effler $29.95 (cloth)
Fashion Illustration Workbooks (4 in series) $8.95 each
Fantasy Art, by Bruce Robertson $24.95 (cloth)
Getting It Printed, by Beach, Shepro & Russon $29.50 (paper)
The Graphic Artist's Guide to Marketing & Self-Promotion, by Sally Prince Davis $15.95 (paper)
The Graphic Arts Studio Manual, by Bert Braham $22.95 (cloth)
Graphic Tools & Techniques, by Laing & Saunders-Davies $24.95 (cloth)
Graphics Handbook, by Howard Munce $14.95 (paper)
Handbook of Pricing & Ethical Guidelines, 7th edition, by The Graphic Artist's Guild $22.95 (paper)
How to Design Trademarks & Logos, by Murphy & Row $24.95 (cloth)
How to Draw & Sell Cartoons, by Ross Thomson & Bill Hewison $18.95 (cloth)
How to Draw & Sell Comic Strips, by Alan McKenzie $18.95 (cloth)
How to Draw Charts & Diagrams, by Bruce Robertson $24.95 (cloth)
How to Understand & Use Design & Layout, by Alan Swann $19.95 (paper)
How to Understand & Use Grids, by Alan Swann $27.95 (cloth)
How to Write and Illustrate Children's Books, edited by Treld Pelkey Bicknell and Felicity Trotman, $22.50 (cloth)
Illustration & Drawing: Styles & Techniques, by Terry Presnall $16.95 (cloth)
Living by Your Brush Alone, by Edna Wagner Piersol $16.95 (paper)
Marker Rendering Techniques, by Dick Powell & Patricia Monahan $32.95 (cloth)

Marker Techniques Workbooks (8 in series) $9.95 each
North Light Dictionary of Art Terms, by Margy Lee Elspass $12.95 (paper)
Papers for Printing, by Mark Beach & Ken Russon $34.50 (paper)
Preparing Your Design for Print, by Lynn John $27.95 (cloth)
Presentation Techniques for the Graphic Artist, by Jenny Mulherin $24.95 (cloth)
Print Production Handbook, by David Bann $16.95 (cloth)
Ready to Use Layouts for Desktop Design, by Chris Prior $27.95 (cloth)
Studio Secrets for the Graphic Artist, by Jack Buchan $29.95 (cloth)
Type: Design, Color, Character & Use, by Michael Beaumont $19.95 (paper)
Using Type Right, by Philip Brady $18.95 (paper)

Watercolor

Basic Watercolor Painting, by Judith Campbell-Reed $16.95 (paper)
Capturing Mood in Watercolor, by Phil Austin, $26.95 (cloth)
Chinese Watercolor Painting: The Four Seasons, by Leslie Tseng-Tseng Yu $24.95 (paper)
Getting Started in Watercolor, by John Blockley $19.95 (paper)
The New Spirit of Watercolor, by Mike Ward $27.95 (cloth)
Painting Nature's Details in Watercolor, by Cathy Johnson $19.95 (paper)
Painting Watercolor Portraits That Glow, by Jan Kunz $27.95 (cloth)
Sir William Russell Flint, edited by Ralph Lewis & Keith Gardner $55.00 (cloth)
Starting with Watercolor, by Rowland Hilder $24.95 (cloth)
Tony Couch Watercolor Techniques Workbook 1 & 2, by Tony Couch $12.95 each (paper)
Watercolor Interpretations, by John Blockley $19.95 (paper)
Watercolor Options, by Ray Loos $22.50 (cloth)
Watercolor Painter's Solution Book, by Angela Gair $24.95 (cloth)
Watercolor—The Creative Experience, by Barbara Nechis $16.95 (paper)
Watercolor Tricks & Techniques, by Cathy Johnson $24.95 (cloth)
Watercolor Workbook, by Bud Biggs & Lois Marshall $19.95 (paper)
Watercolor: You Can Do It!, by Tony Couch $26.95 (cloth)
Webb on Watercolor, by Frank Webb $29.95 (cloth)

Watercolor Videos

Big Brush Watercolor, with Ron Ranson $29.95 (VHS only)
Watercolor Fast & Loose, with Ron Ranson $29.95 (VHS or Beta)
Watercolor Pure & Simple, with Ron Ranson $29.95 (VHS or Beta)

Mixed Media

The Art of Scratchboard, by Cecile Curtis $23.95 (cloth)
Calligraphy Workbooks (4 in series) $7.95 each

Catching Light in Your Paintings, by Charles Sovek $18.95 (paper)
Colored Pencil Drawing Techniques, by Iain Hutton-Jamieson $24.95 (cloth)
Complete Guide to Fashion Illustration, by Colin Barnes $32.95 (cloth)
The Complete Oil Painting Book, by Wendon Blake $29.95 (cloth)
Drawing & Painting with Ink, by Fritz Henning $24.95 (cloth)
Drawing for Pleasure, edited by Peter D. Johnson $15.95 (paper)
Drawing Workbooks (4 in series) $8.95 each
Exploring Color, by Nita Leland $19.95 (paper)
The Figure, edited by Walt Reed $16.95 (paper)
Keys to Drawing, by Bert Dodson $19.95 (paper)
Light: How to See It, How to Paint It, by Lucy Willis $24.95 (cloth)
Make Your Own Picture Frames, by Jenny Rodwell $12.95 (paper)
Mixing Color, by Jeremy Galton $24.95 (cloth)
The North Light Handbook of Artist's Materials, by Ian Hebblewhite $24.95 (cloth)
The North Light Illustrated Book of Painting Techniques, by Elizabeth Tate $27.95 (cloth)
Oil Painting: A Direct Approach, by Joyce Pike $26.95 (cloth)
Painting Birds & Animals, by Patricia Monahan $21.95 (cloth)
Painting in Oils, edited by Michael Bowers $18.95 (cloth)
Painting Murals, by Patricia Seligman $26.95 (cloth)
Painting Seascapes in Sharp Focus, by Lin Seslar $19.95 (paper)
Painting with Acrylics, by Jenny Rodwell $19.95 (paper)
Painting with Oils, by Patricia Monahan $19.95 (cloth)
Painting with Pastels, edited by Peter D. Johnson $16.95 (paper)
Pastel Painting Techniques, by Guy Roddon $24.95 (cloth)
The Pencil, by Paul Calle $17.95 (paper)
People Painting Scrapbook, by J. Everett Draper $26.95 (cloth)
Perspective in Art, by Michael Woods $13.95 (paper)
Perspective Without Pain Workbooks (4 in series) $9.95 each
Photographing Your Artwork, by Russell Hart $16.95 (paper)
Putting People in Your Paintings, by J. Everett Draper $22.50 (cloth)
Tonal Values: How to See Them, How to Paint Them, by Angela Gair $24.95 (cloth)

To order directly from the publisher, include $3.00 postage and handling for one book, $1.00 for each additional book. Allow 30 days for delivery.

North Light Books
1507 Dana Avenue,
Cincinnati, Ohio 45207

Credit card orders
Call TOLL-FREE
1-800-289-0963
Prices subject to change without notice.